101 FAQs about Coaching

Maggie João

authorHOUSE®

AuthorHouse™ UK Ltd.
500 Avebury Boulevard
Central Milton Keynes, MK9 2BE
www.authorhouse.co.uk
Phone: 08001974150

First published by AuthorHouse   07/12/2011

ISBN: 978-1-4567-7398-4

To all fellow coaches:

May your journey be as authentic and wonderful as you have envisioned.

About the Author

Maggie João is an Executive and Life Coach accredited by the International Institute of Coaching and the Academy of Executive Coaching. She heads the International Institute of Coaching in Portugal. She is also a writer.

Before running her own coaching practice, her business background consisted of ten successful years in Manufacturing and Supply Chain with various global organisations within the auto, food and services sector. She has travelled the world and lived in 12 countries.

With clients in three continents, Maggie practises non-directive and non-judgmental coaching in English, Portuguese and Spanish. To contact Maggie, please email: maggie.joao@coachinglife.eu.

Acknowledgements

This book would not have been possible without the continuous support of my precious friends, Lena di Gurgana and Jon D'augaarda. They have been with me every single step of the way and have given me the strength to make this book a reality.

I would also like to send huge thanks to my family, especially my mum, dad, and second parents, for their permanent support. A special thank you goes to my sister Cristina João and to Ana Elisabete Pires, for their encouragement and kind words of support.

A big hug goes to my truthful friends, Patricia Edvarsson and Johan Cundy, for their support throughout the years. A special hug goes to Alex Guillaume and Yulia Osoyanu, who have been wonderful friends and are always there when needed.

Thank you to all my first reviewers, whose invaluable feedback has helped me shape this book into its final form. I also would like to give my deepest appreciation to Katherine Tulpa and John Leary-Joyce for writing such interesting forewords.

I would like to thank my editor, Victoria Ipri of *The Confident Copywriter*, for her patience, suggestions and comments on my work. A deep thank you goes to my friend Judy Barber, herself a coach and author, who supported me through the editing phase. Without you, this project would have surely been more difficult.

Last but not least, a big thank you to all my fellow coaches and clients who, one way or the other, have shaped this book. Our interactions have built my coaching career and brought me to where I am today. For that I am truly grateful. There is no other place I would rather be.

To the readers who wish to send me feedback and comments about the book and to ask me questions about coaching, please contact me via my webpage www.coachinglife.eu or email me at maggie.joao@coachinglife.eu. Thank you!

Contents

Foreword   xv

Preamble   xvii

Introduction   xix

PART I – ADMINISTRATIVE ASPECTS OF COACHING   1

1. What is coaching?   3

2. What are today's core coaching categories?   5

3. What are the benefits of coaching?   7

4. What are the differences between coaching and mentoring?   9

5. What are the differences between coaching and psychotherapy?   11

6. Where can coaching be useful?   13

7. How can I become a coach?   15

8. Which is the best institution to choose for obtaining a coaching diploma? 17

9. Who can become a coach?   19

10. What is entailed in the preparation phase of a coaching session?   21

11. How should a coach prepare spiritually and emotionally for a coaching session? 23

12. Where is the best place to have a coaching session?   25

13. How long should a coaching session last?   27

14. How long should a coaching engagement last?   29

15. How important is a coaching code of ethics?   31

16. How do you treat confidentiality within a coaching context?   35

17. Why is accreditation useful?   37

18. Who dictates the coaching industry standards?   39

19. What should be included in a coaching contract?   41

20. What is the best policy for managing last minute cancellations?   43

21. How much should coaches charge for coaching sessions?   45

22. What is coaching supervision?   47

23. Where can coaching supervision be found?   49

24. Why should a coach be coached?   51

25. How do referrals work?   53

26. What is the impact of a testimonial?   55

27. When should I pursue further development in my coaching career?   57

28. How do I know which coaching books to read?   59

29. How is the benefit-cost ratio calculated?   61

30. How can behavioural improvements be assessed?   63

31. Why is evaluation of a coaching engagement necessary?   65

32. What restrictions are there regarding coaching family
     members and friends?   67

PART II – CORE ASPECTS OF THE COACHING PRACTICE   69

33. What are the most common mistakes coaches make?   71

34. What is the best coaching model to follow?   73

35. Must all coaching sessions begin with goal setting?   75

36. What are the most common mistakes in goal-setting?   77

37. How can you help clients go from dream list to goal list?   81

38. How can I ensure I am ready with the next question once the client has finished
     talking?   83

39. How long should I wait before asking another question?   85

40. How do I keep my attention focused?   87

41. What is the best way to remember what the client just said?   89

42. How can the coach refocus his or her attention once concentration is lost? 91

43. In an executive coaching context, what should be reported back to the sponsor? 93

44. What can I do to maximise learning?   95

45. Where can I learn more about coaching and related practices?   97

46. How can NLP enrich coaching?   99

47. What are clean language questions and when should they be asked?   101

48. Which is better, face-to-face coaching or telephone coaching?   103

49. What are my coaching values?   105

50. How important is it to be clear about my own 'forbidden territories'?　107

51. Who can help me practise coaching?　109

52. At the beginning of a session, what should I mention about contracting?　111

53. What is the best policy regarding taking notes during a coaching session?　113

54. What should I do when the session is running over time?　115

55. What are the different kinds of questions I could use in coaching sessions?　117

56. When is it useful to ask closed questions during a coaching session?　119

57. What type of questions should I avoid in a coaching session?　121

58. What type of homework is it advisable to request in a session?　123

59. How do I close a coaching session?　125

60. What can I do if my client becomes highly emotional during a session?　127

61. What can I do when my client keeps answering "I don't know" to my questions?　129

62. What can I do if I don't feel comfortable tackling a specific subject with a client?　131

63. How can my internal dialogue be silenced?　133

64. What else should I watch for during a coaching session?　135

65. How can I build rapport with my clients without mimicking them?　137

66. When is the right time to terminate the coach-client relationship?　139

67. How can I ensure the best outcome for a coaching session?　141

68. Where do you draw the line between client confidentiality and moral obligation?　143

69. What are the most empowering methods of changing limiting beliefs?　145

70. How can I help clients define new beliefs?　147

71. What contributes to self-esteem?　149

72. What methods can be used to overcome low self-esteem?　151

73. What are the best ways to explore clients' metaphors?　153

74. How effective is scaling?　157

75. How can I improve my coaching skills?　159

76. What do you do with difficult clients?　161

77. What safeguards must I take when coaching minors?　163

78. How can I express my intuition in a coaching session?　165

79. What is self-coaching?　167

80. Who am I as a coach?　169

81. How do I coach?   171

82. What stretches me as a coach?   173

83. How can I become the best coach I possibly can?   175

PART III – TIPS FOR GROWING YOUR COACHING BUSINESS   177

84. How can I define my coaching niche?   179

85. Who could my clients be?   181

86. What are my clients looking for?   183

87. Which are the best strategies for creating my coaching profile?   185

88. What are the best techniques for finding new coaching clients?   187

89. How can I promote my coaching business?   189

90. What are the most common marketing traps for coaching businesses?   191

91. What are the most common coaching packages and offers?   193

92. What other services can I offer apart from coaching sessions?   195

93. Who can help me grow my business?   199

94. From whom can I drawn inspiration for building my coaching practice?   201

95. What are the advantages and disadvantages of a partnership?   203

96. When should I stop practising pro-bono coaching?   205

97. How can I keep my business costs down?   207

98. How far down the line is the best time to increase my coaching rates?   211

99. How can I keep my focus when coaching in a recession?   213

100. When does 'going international' become appropriate?   215

101. What is the best approach to building my coaching business?   217

Appendix   219

Bibliography   221

Index   223

Foreword

Coaching is now at an encouraging stage of growth, evolving from an industry to a young profession. What this book brings is a level of depth and richness, with knowledge and contributions from a number of areas, including evidence based research from academia; guidelines and best practice materials from professional coaching bodies; various models and approaches from providers and trainers of coaching; and practical tips and insights from coaches themselves.

It is this last category, written by a practising coach and from a practical view point that makes this book so refreshing. Maggie João firstly asks all the questions that many coaches, particularly those going into coaching for the first time so often ask, and does this in a way that captures the true *essence* of coaching at the most fundamental level. Greater still, she does this in a real conversational style that makes it fully inviting for any new or experienced coach.

While the highlights of *101 FAQs about Coaching* are the examples and straight forward responses following each question, I will leave it the readers to enjoy these as they read through the pages. However, as a pre-curser, I have summarised below a number of the key themes that emerge for me.

Knowing Oneself

"Who am I as coach?" is probably one of the most profound questions a coach can ask him/herself. The more we become aware of what drives and motivates us, the stronger a coach we become. This can also help us articulate our strengths and offerings to prospective clients in a way that is authentic and which gives us the most energy - thereby having a positive effect on the coaching relationship.

Sincerity and Honesty

A thread throughout this book is about coaches being honest and sincere. This helps us build deeper levels of trust both in the relationship with ourselves and with our clients. It also role models coach-like behaviours, as well as leadership. In other words, we are walking the talk and reinforcing the qualities we hope to see from others that we coach or aim to influence.

Taking Responsibility

"What are your boundaries as a coach, and what ethics do you subscribe to?" There is a duty of care for a coach to take responsibility to protect their clients. This means understanding the limits of his training, knowing when to end a client relationship, and when it is appropriate to refer someone on when the clients' needs cross into areas they are not qualified in (e.g. counselling).

Ongoing Professional Development

The development of a coach doesn't stop after initial coach training: it is ongoing. There are a number of options out there for a coach to expand their knowledge and sharpen what they do. This includes coach supervision - a requirement for those who are members of a professional body and striving for accreditation - as well as CPD (Continuing Professional Development) events, seminars, and conferences; reading coaching related journals and publications; or even participating in online discussion forums to gain perspectives and approaches from other peers/coaches

Being Flexible

As much as we may aim to get out of the way in a coaching session so that we can remain objective with our clients, we undoubtedly bring ourselves into our coaching. The values exercise mentioned in question 49 is a very useful way to better understand our biases or triggers that can influence a coaching relationship. This can help us remain more open to our client's "map of the world". There are also useful tips to reduce internal dialogue so that we are listening on much deeper level - and less attached - and so that we are able to be more flexible to the needs of our client in the "third person" view.

Aspiring for Excellence

In Maggie's own words, I love the question, "How can I become the best coach I possibly can?" A self-aware coach, who is responsible, aware of his or her areas of competence (as well as limitations), will also have a strong desire for excellence. They challenge the status quo, and hold the bar high both personally and with their clients. This is what makes the difference between a good coach and a great coach, and they never stop looking at ways to up their game.

The above are my key takeaways from the wisdom Maggie so generously shares with us. What makes this evolving profession so dynamic is that we are not only on a continuous learning journey to develop and advance our practices, but also on a journey to collaborate and learn together in pursuit of coaching excellence. On this note I encourage you, following the reading of this book, to

1. Reflect;

2. Decide what's most useful for you at this juncture of your coaching, and

3. Take action on some of the insights gained.

And most importantly, to continue to *ask the questions* - which the author so clearly role models here - that others may not dare to ask. It is this art of asking incisive questions that enables us, our clients, and arguably our profession to grow to the fullest potential.

Katherine Tulpa
Global CEO, Association for Coaching

Preamble

Coaching is now firmly established as a rich people development activity. When I launched the Academy of Executive Coaching (AoEC) in 2000 an article in the Harvard Business Review aptly described the coaching world as being like the "Wild West".

The last 10 years have seen enormous strides in establishing the ethics, standards and definitions for coaching. The professional bodies in collaboration with the training organisations like the AoEC, which Maggie talks about in the book, have now created a strong system of accreditation and self-regulation.

There are many books and articles on the depth and complexity of coaching and the coaching relationship. Maggie has drawn on her own personal and professional journey to create a very accessible and straightforward route into addressing the basic but essential questions that face the enquirer or newly qualified coach.

In providing such a concise explanation she opens the door for the budding coach to explore the numerous avenues that will inform their on-going coach development.

This book is timely and valuable contribution to the evolution of the profession.

John Leary-Joyce
CEO of the AoEC
President of the EMCC UK, European Mentoring & Coaching Council

Introduction

I was introduced to coaching many years ago while doing a full-time job. I have understood for some time that people have the answers within themselves and are, in fact, *the* answer to many problems that occur in their professional and personal lives. I've always been passionate about helping others and about writing. Coaching fulfils both passions – helping me to help others through reflection, challenge and support, and allowing me to dive into the world of writing. For me coaching is the perfect fit.

The book is a repository of the essential aspects of coaching, a profession which is still far from being fully regulated. Many organisations provide standards of excellence to ensure high quality coaching. These standards offer a great deal of support and help. However, throughout my career, few have been the times when colleagues and I found all the relevant information in one place. I often had to buy several different books and search dozens of different websites to get acquainted with the scattered information about the coaching industry.

101 FAQs about Coaching is the result of extensive research and consultation with other coaches with different levels of experience, career paths, and nationalities. This book discusses questions and doubts about:

- Administrative issues affecting coaches;
- Day to day challenges;
- Issues affecting business growth.

The way this book is structured allows the reader to consult specific questions and answers without the need to read the whole of the book in one go. All relevant points are highlighted on each question and answer. However, for thorough understanding I recommended that you read the book from start to finish, at your own pace.

A book about coaching that contains the answers to these common challenges minimises both research and time for many coaches - time which could be spent practising coaching skills that make a difference in their professional journey. Hence this book became alive in my mind. After taking the difficult steps of self-discipline, organisation and determination, the creation of these pages is a dream come true.

Throughout the book the client and the coach are predominantly referred to as male, solely for simplicity. This by no means indicates any preference.

Nothing is perfect and improvements come through the support of others. Therefore I invite you to provide authentic and direct feedback. Your comments and questions will contribute to an improved 2nd edition. Thank you in advance for your feedback and continuous support! Please visit my website www.coachinglife.eu or email me at maggie.joao@coachinglife.eu.

Part I – Administrative Aspects of Coaching

All aspiring coaches have concerns and doubts about the most efficient methods of building a practice. Accreditation, supervision, ethics and choosing a meeting location are just a few of those concerns. This chapter will address these and other common challenges and offer solutions.

1. What is coaching?

Different sources define coaching as a new profession, an industry yet to be fully regulated and another personal development stream. Some call it a process, some a methodology and some a way of thinking. Nevertheless all sources agree on the benefits coaching brings to individuals, whether in a professional or personal context. The answer to question 3 addresses these benefits in greater detail.

From my point of view coaching is simply an interaction between two individuals. One acts as listener while the other is the speaker. The listener is the coach and the speaker is the client or coachee. The objective behind such interaction is to help the client structure his thinking process regarding a specific subject. It's most likely the basis of a problem, issue or dilemma at that moment in time. Besides structuring the thinking process, sessions clarify doubts the coachee has in relation to the topic he would like to discuss. Through this interaction choices are developed and revealed. Plans are created in order to help the client move forward toward his personal and professional goals.

The interesting points about the coaching interaction are the ease and speed of reaching a solution. This is a much easier and faster process than doing it without any source of support.

On another note, the topic brought up by the client needn't necessarily be a problem, issue or dilemma, nor need it be in the present. The issue may centre on future objectives the individual wishes to reach, other ways to sustain an already fulfilling personal relationship or how to further improve business management skills. Whatever the subject, it is important to the client. It is the coach's responsibility to focus his attention on the client's agenda to achieve the best outcome.

Having said this, it is also crucial to understand where the coach's boundaries lie and which subjects may interfere with partiality. We will look into this in more detail with questions 50 and 62.

Additionally interaction between coach and client can follow a specific process or methodology. This can be helpful when conducting the session. However, good coaching practices exclude:

- Advising;
- Leading the client to certain conclusions;
- Assuming what the client has/has not said;
- Clinging to the client after the issue has been resolved.

Hence it is advisable for the coach to create a safe networking environment for himself through supervision, co-coaching and other support. It is also important to remain up-to-date with the latest industry tools and best practice.

Coaching is a journey of self-discovery that unleashes the individual's potential, transforming dreams into reality. As with all such ventures, the essential ingredients for success are sincerity and honesty. They are the basis upon which one can build trust and confidence in the relationship. If not in place, then the process will not reach its full potential and will lack the steam to succeed.

Mastering several tools and skills is necessary and will be discussed throughout these pages.

2. What are today's core coaching categories?

Dozens of coaching niches have been created in recent years to meet public demand. From fashion to parenting, de-cluttering to motherhood, business to weight loss, coaching comes in many sizes and shapes, but always with the same theme: helping others live happier and better balanced lives. Niches are specialisations that fall into one of the following coaching main categories:

- Life Coaching;
- Executive Coaching;
- Business Coaching.

These categories can intertwine and they do so quite regularly. Topics discussed in a life coaching session, for example, may spill over into the coachee's professional life, and vice versa. The most common topics discussed in a coaching context are linked with life challenges, such as self-esteem, self-confidence, work-life balance issues or the quest for life's purpose and meaning.

Life Coaching applies to personal matters: relationships, values, self-esteem, stress, and so on. This type of coaching is provided on a one-to-one basis and includes niches such as fashion, motherhood, health and parenting, de-cluttering and weight loss.

Executive coaching is directed to middle and top corporate management but also applies to politicians and diplomats. It is also a one-to-one approach, but payment tends to be made by the employer of the individual receiving the coaching rather than the individual himself (although there are exceptions). Topics normally covered are team relationships, leadership issues, goal setting and career values. Ethical coaching and corporate coaching (coaching a team/department within a company) are considered as niches within executive coaching.

Business coaching is about coaching a business to improve its sales, reduce costs, create customer loyalty programmes, promotional packages etc. In this case the coachees are heads of departments or perhaps even the CEO. In some cases, for instance when coaching the managing director, there is a fine line between executive coaching and business coaching.

It is in the business coaching category that we find *franchising coaching*. The coach buys his franchise licence in exchange for templates, processes and methodologies which dictate the way he will help the businesses. Whilst there is some value in this type of coaching, personally I believe it to be more a consultancy type of role than authentic coaching.

Again one can find dozens of different coaching niches out there. What to choose from: becoming a fashion coach, a weight loss coach, an executive coach or a business coach? The answer is to uncover where your passion lies. I am sure you will shine once you follow the route that unleashes your potential. Honest reflection is required for getting the perfect answer.

Delivery of coaching services can be provided in different ways. Traditional face-to-face meetings offer the coach several sources of information about the client's state of mind through listening, observation and intuition.

However developments in technology mean that telephone and Internet coaching are becoming the preferred option. In fact studies reveal that 90% of life coaching is done using distant means of communication such as telephone, online chat rooms, *Skype* and email. Despite the fact that coaching is then provided in one dimension, for instance, visual (via email or online chatting) or auditory (via telephone), there are certain advantages to it (see question 48). Notice that enabling web cameras when *Skyping* combines visual and sound dimensions. Each communication method offers different benefits and one or more may fit your style and that of your client. As the coach, you may benefit from familiarising yourself with all the methods of communication so as to best fit your client's needs.

3. What are the benefits of coaching?

Coaching is a support system that offers the coachee a long list of benefits for meeting the overall goals of happiness and balance:

- Self-discovery;
- Paradigm shift in emergent issues;
- Clearing the way to restructuring the thinking process;
- Removing fears and phobias;
- Positively impacting limiting personal beliefs;
- Looking at problems as opportunities;
- Developing creativity;
- Creating a positive attitude;
- Challenging thinking patterns;
- Connecting two or more events that seem unrelated;
- Improving self-esteem and self-confidence;
- Identifying options towards resolution;
- Creating action plans;
- Attaining objectives;
- Promoting a healthy and safe debate.

Through the coaching interaction powerful questions asked by the coach will guide the client toward self-discovery, help to move the client away from unfounded fears and phobias and empower their beliefs. It begins with shifting the client's thinking patterns.

The trust developed by the coachee towards the coach allows him or her to feel safe during this transition. The coach knows enough interesting exercises to challenge the client to see the issue from different perspectives and this tests old thinking patterns.

It is not unusual that as a result of a coaching session, the coachee can link two events which seemed impossible to connect until that very moment. Additionally, improving his self-esteem (his own view of how much he is worth) and self-confidence (his own view of how much he knows about a specific subject) is another of the benefits coaching provides. The coachee leaves a session feeling re-energised, happy, confident and ready to move forward.

Certainly the client will have identified several options for resolving his issues. Not all coaching is about an issue or a problem. More often than not the topic is a positive challenge and the client would like to strengthen or think through aspects of this challenge in order to achieve greater success. When it comes to creating options, coaches João Alberto Catalão and Ana Penim highlight that:

- One option equals an obligation;
- Two options equals a dilemma;
- Three or more options generate freedom of choice.

Hence it is always helpful to assist the client in generating three or more options. In this context, the question "What else?" is very useful.

With several options identified it will be easy to assess which the client would like to take action upon first. Then the coach can help him create his own action plan. This plan would include:

1. Actions;

2. Dates for implementation;

3. Support or resources required;

4. Contingency plans for getting around obstacles.

Inevitably coaching helps the client reach the goal or objective that brought him to coaching in the first place. These goals and objectives range from brainstorming ideas to resolving complex emotional situations. Examples are, "How can I feel unblocked when talking to my boss?" and "How can I be happy again in my marriage?"

Alongside these benefits, coaching is a healthy and safe place to open up and debate issues which the client may feel are inappropriate to discuss among friends, family members or others. Coaching is based on mutual, authentic trust and honesty. It offers a safe harbour where the client can open up and share his view of the world, without the fear of judgement, retribution, or preconceived ideas.

Truly coaching is a rewarding journey for both coach and client.

4. What are the differences between coaching and mentoring?

Coaching is often confused with mentoring. While both practices improve individual performance and the attainment of professional objectives, there are several differences.

Mentoring assumes the mentor has vast levels of experience in the coachee's field of business. Very often a mentor is someone quite senior who works for the same organisation, perhaps in a different department.

Coaching, on the other hand, is often practised by someone from outside the organisation, although more and more companies are building up their own in-house coaching departments to ensure the company's culture is embedded in the coaching sessions and, obviously, to reduce costs.

Coaching does not require the coach be experienced in the client's industry. In fact sometimes this is an obstacle.

Mentors draw inspiration from their own experiences and methods whilst coaches challenge thinking patterns, allowing clients to visualise different roads to their destinations.

Mentors are quick to give advice and lead the individual towards given solutions. In some cases this may fall short of taking the steps which might really unleash the individual's potential. Coaching, on the contrary, isn't advisory. Coaching unfolds on the spot, based on the client's expression of feelings and emotions.

Although unusual, it can happen that manipulation takes place during mentoring. The mentor may advise the individual on the basis of decisions previously taken by the directors. On that basis the individual's concerns may be far from the top of the priority list. The heart of the coaching relationship lies with the coach and coachee. Despite the fact that within an executive coaching environment the relationship is threefold (coach, individual and sponsor/employer), the coach's ultimate loyalty remains with the coachee.

Mentoring is essential to the growth of an individual within an organisation, allowing him to understand company politics and nuances which coaching may not be able to achieve.

Both coaching and mentoring are important practices, the main objective of which is the development of the individual to enhance performance. Mentors can apply coaching competencies. The contrary is seldom true.

5. What are the differences between coaching and psychotherapy?

Noble Manhattan Coaching, one of Europe's leading coach training organisations, summarises the differences between coaching and psychotherapy in the table below:

Coaching	Psychotherapy
Coaching sessions are provided through face-to-face meetings, phone and the Internet.	Psychotherapy session is a face-to-face meeting.
Coaching focuses on the present and the future.	Psychotherapy focuses mainly on past issues.
Coaching is for functional people who want to enhance personal and professional life.	Psychotherapy is for dysfunctional people who want to become functional.
Coaching tackles all type of topics in the personal and professional fields.	Psychotherapy is very much focussed on the personal matters of the individual.
Coaching reinforces new positive behaviours and attitudes.	Psychotherapy explores the causes for the problems the client is facing.
Coaching does not centre the session on the problem, but rather on the client.	The session is centred on the problem.
Coaching is pro-active and ignites the client's initiative to look for solutions to their issues.	Psychotherapy is reactive, exploring problems and attitudes once they come up.
Coaching helps the client define clear objectives and find different thinking patterns to create several options.	Psychotherapy explores the client's feelings and emotions linked with their fear and phobias.

What coaching and psychotherapy have in common are that they are prejudice-free, focused on the client's agenda and use similar competencies and skills, such as active listening, powerful questions, exploration of metaphors and building rapport.

For both practices it is fundamental to create a high level of trust and honesty between practitioner and client in order to be most effective and productive.

Both coaching and psychotherapy help the individual to become more self-conscious and to discover himself, as well as to modify his internal dialogue as a more positive and effective self-help tool.

In some instances psychotherapy offers a better support system for the individual. The coach must acknowledge when he is out of his depth and refer the client to this more appropriate type of support. On the other hand, it is not unusual to hear someone talking about the need to get psychological help when, in fact, what they might really need is a coach.

6. Where can coaching be useful?

Coaching helps the individual in his personal and professional worlds. The list below is not exhaustive but it covers areas where coaching has achieved excellent results:

- Adolescents and young offenders;
- Advisory;
- Improving business results;
- Career change;
- Conflict resolution;
- Consultancy;
- Continuous improvement;
- (Early) retirement;
- Education;
- De-cluttering;
- First time motherhood;
- Healthcare;
- Management;
- Marketing;
- Mentoring;
- Parenting;
- Performance appraisal;
- Personal styling;
- Recruitment and interviewing;
- Redundancy;
- Relocation;
- Sales;
- Spiritual development;
- Team Building;
- Training;
- Turnaround management;
- Weight loss and fitness;
- Work-Life balance.

These aren't necessarily coaching niches but they are areas where coaching can be applied and bring positive change.

In each of these fields, coaching can be applied in various intensities. One can run coaching sessions in these fields and apply coaching principles, exercises and tools. Each situation will dictate the best approach.

Nevertheless, through adequate guidance and applying excellent skills coaching can open doors to unleash one's potential, creating options that resonate with the coachee's values, and result in a desired and achievable outcome.

7. How can I become a coach?

There is more to becoming a coach than simply waking up one day and affirming, "I am a coach". The future coach has to accumulate through appropriate qualifications a solid background of coaching skills, models and experiences to deepen his knowledge.

Finding the most suitable school or institution that provides coaching diplomas is the tricky part. Internet search engines, such as Google, are good sources of information, as well as relevant magazines.

There are several coaching qualifications on offer and it can be quite stressful making a decision. When it comes to advertisements, such as "full coaching qualification in 1 day", I seriously doubt the validity of the course!

When choosing a training institution, please bear in mind the following:

- **Length of programme** – Is it one week, several months? Does it sound right to you? Does it fit with your personal schedule?
- **Distance or face-to-face learning** – Don't dismiss the relevance of the learning experience with fellow colleagues;
- **Accreditation** – Which body certifies this programme? What is the process for attaining accreditation after course completion?
- **Price and promotions** – Beware that when the discount is too great, the value of the product may be too little;
- **Evaluation process** – How will you be evaluated? No testing may be appealing, but how will you know for sure that you have the necessary knowledge? How will the training company know you have embraced your education? Some evaluation processes are far too complex and difficult. Be smart and make the choice that is right for you;
- **After diploma services** – What type of services are provided after graduation and course completion?

Even though many purchases in life are based on price and convenience, take time to reflect rather than making a decision lightly.

After completing your diploma you are basically on your own, especially if you don't have an institution supporting you. When you step into the business world it is important to show credibility, knowledge and success. This is when accreditation becomes an advantage.

8. Which is the best institution to choose for obtaining a coaching diploma?

The criteria for selecting a coaching school depend on what you wish to achieve. What type of coaching niche do you wish to pursue? How long you wish to spend studying? How important is customer service after you complete your studies? What is the accreditation process?

For some students the name of an award-winning school listed on his or her curriculum vitae is a must, whilst for others an easier accreditation process is top of their list.

Other important criteria for a good programme include theory input, skills practice, feedback, practice supervision, support building practice, graduate network, course accreditation and academic standards.

There are plenty of coaching organisations which want your money and which have millions of tempting but tricky marketing campaigns. Don't fall for anything without a thorough check of the company's reputation. Also, when the evaluation process is too simple, be suspicious of the integrity of the entire learning circle.

I suggest you browse the Internet, phone a few coaching organisations and ask for their course brochures in advance. You can also attend a one-day or weekend seminar, which normally tends to be free or low cost. Usually the school's most prominent members attend - either the CEO or a highly recommended tutor. You can have a conversation and clarify some points. Afterwards, in the comfort of your home, and after having time to consult people whose opinions you value, make your decision.

Don't make price the sole criteria for selection even though prices vary significantly. There are certainly lots of expensive courses that don't match cost with teaching competence. There are others with attractive low prices, but their materials fall short of expectations.

In the process of selecting an accredited coaching institution, weigh up all the options. You will be the one reading through the school's materials and contacting people with questions and further support, so be certain you are happy with your choice.

9. Who can become a coach?

Basically, anyone can become a coach, regardless of previous educational background and professional experience. While it is important for credibility to have a previous profession and education, it is not compulsory.

People turn to a coach for answers to their problems. Not that the coach will have all the answers, but the practitioner has the opportunity to ask powerful questions, to challenge and support, in a way that provides a structured thinking process, defies old perceptions that block performance improvement, and allows the individual to create options for achieving their desired outcomes.

The skills required for effective coaching, such as active listening, questioning, building rapport, using intuition, providing feedback, exploring metaphors and values elicitation, are all qualities that can be developed over time. Hence, with proper guidance, anyone can study and become excellent in these skills.

However, not all will excel in the coaching profession. Why, you may ask? The answer lies in personal passion. If your heart is in the process you will be on the road to success. Determination and discipline are also essential ingredients for becoming an acknowledged coach.

What the coaching relationship needs most of all is the bond of trust and honesty between two people. The client must feel safe to open his heart and share confidences. You don't need a special coaching course for that, though it is required in the business context when sponsors and organisations request proof of knowledge and credibility, such as qualification and accreditation certificates.

Years of previous professional experience are not a requirement for practising coaching. One does not need to be an expert in a specific field to coach another person. However, I recognise the advantage of having previous professional experience or other higher qualifications since such experience grants rapid thinking processes, logic and knowledge of various terminologies to the coach. Therefore it is common to come across coaches who were once engineers, salesmen, nurses and managers. They draw inspiration from their past experiences and education for coming closer to the client's reality and challenges. It can be a bridge between them.

For executive coach Ana Paula Nacif, *"leadership should not be confined to the realm of corporate or executive coaching. Leadership is every coach's business. (...) As coaches, if we want to serve our clients to the best of our ability, we need to master leadership. (...) It is not about doing, but being".*

More important than accreditation and paper qualifications are *walking the talk* and truly understanding the struggles a client faces.

10. What is entailed in the preparation phase of a coaching session?

Preparing for a session is an essential task for the coach prior to any coaching meeting, whether over the phone, by internet or face-to-face, in order to achieve a successful session.

Preparation involves both the physical surroundings and the spiritual state. Numerous recommendations can be found for physical preparation. A few are listed below:

- Clear the desk or room where the coaching session will take place to avoid any source of distraction;
- If necessary have a "not to be disturbed" sign on the door;
- Go to the bathroom ahead of the session;
- Have a glass of water handy during the session;
- Switch off all sources of noise, such as radio/TV, telephone, fax, mobiles and other electronic equipment that makes disturbing sounds.

'Spiritual preparation', such as deep breathing, meditation and lighting candles, helps the coach clear his mind from his own issues, so that he is better equipped to conduct a session fully focused on the client's agenda.

Some people are very fond of *Mindfulness Meditation*, which differs from concentration. Concentration involves the practitioner focusing his attention on an object. In mindfulness meditation every aspect of the experience is welcomed and appreciated. With mindfulness meditation the practitioner takes on the role of an impartial observer of everything that occurs around him in the present moment. His intention is not focused, but mindful - fully aware and awake - to what is going on. The breath can be used as an anchor to the present moment in mindfulness meditation, but apart from that no attempt is made to direct attention. Whatever thoughts, distractions, sounds, images, ideas, or feelings arise, nothing is excluded. Everything is welcomed. Simply pay attention to whatever is there. Don't judge or evaluate – that is definitely linked with the principles of coaching!

The two main risks of unsuccessful preparation are clearly:

1. Listening at an inappropriate level (level one - internal listening)[1];

2. Being judgmental.

By contrast, when listening at level two and three (focused listening and global listening, respectively - the advised levels for listening in a coaching session), the focus is on the client, his body language and feelings. The coach's intuition and sensing is at full capacity, enabling the interpretation of tone of voice, pace, excuses, hesitation and resistance, labels, reluctance, lack of motivation and/or enthusiasm. Coaches also appropriately challenge limiting beliefs, criticism and any information gaps in the client's speech - not to mention that the coach should be totally focused on the coachee's agenda and ultimately on helping him achieve the desired goal.

Therefore, preparation is vital for a good start to a session. As Benjamin Franklin said, *"Failing to prepare is preparing to fail."*

---

1. There are three levels of listening: internal listening; focused listening and global listening. These are associated to a descending activity of self-talk and an ascending use of intuition and observation.

11. How should a coach prepare spiritually and emotionally for a coaching session?

Preparing for a coaching session is a necessary task, but plenty of coaches rush through this step.

In my view, spiritual and emotional preparation is a must before conducting a session. Your spirit as a coach must be free of dark emotions, such as anger, hatred, frustration, sadness, and of overwhelming emotions like excitement. Then you are better equipped to truly focus on what your client is saying and conveying through body language, sounds, silences, breathing patterns etc. You are present in the room in a passive, discrete manner.

Entering the session irritated about your own problems, feeling moody about the state of the world, feeling sad, or in any other way being preoccupied with your own feelings cannot create the atmosphere necessary for a successful session.

We all know that coaching is about the individual, not the coach. So ask yourself, why would the coach's mood impact the session itself? The fact is that people's moods influence everything around them, even when the interaction is very basic. The unconscious mind behaves in ways that, even though invisible, can cast impressions on others for eternity. Hence, it is only sensible to prepare yourself adequately before a session. However, don't try to eliminate your personality from the equation. Your clients are paying for your signature presence, your energy and your way of doing things.

Experienced coaches advise a minimum of 20 minutes' preparation before any session, with silence and no distractions.

Meditation can also be very important. The power of meditation is enormous. It calms your spirit and offers a balance between *here and now* and *there and then*. I strongly recommend you follow-up on this topic. Read more about the benefits of meditation.

Another way of preparing is through yoga. Whilst this works when you work from home and your session will be done over the phone or Internet, it may not be applicable when meeting clients elsewhere.

There are no one-size-fits-all spiritual and emotional preparation tips. What works for you may not work for your colleagues. Try out several options, and then decide for what works best for you.

It is important to choose something that calms you down, silences your internal dialogue and that can be triggered anywhere to help you be effective in a matter of moments.

12. Where is the best place to have a coaching session?

Every textbook about coaching mentions that sessions should be conducted in a quiet place where the client feels safe to express his emotions, open up his heart and talk about his fears and beliefs.

Some coaches advise having the coaching session in a hired room with minimal decorations and away from curious eyes in order to prevent distractions in the thinking process. Others believe that, within the context of working for an organisation, the sessions are better conducted on the organisation premises.

All of this is valid. Nonetheless, coaching can take many forms and shapes. It can take place in dentists' waiting rooms, at a supermarket, in a bar, on an airplane or in an elevator. It only takes a powerful question to help the individual think outside of the box and alter old thinking patterns or to facilitate the exploration of other options that have been invisible. The power of good questioning doesn't depend on time limits or borders. Even though some meetings aren't really classified as coaching sessions, all situations can be considered when coaching. How many times have you opened up to your best friend on a bus, a noisy coffee shop, during your shopping spree or when walking on the street? However for best results, I recommend that you are fully focussed on the speaker or the client in order to observe body language, word patterns and intonation. Keep eye contact and express your intuition.

This takes us to a very important point - self-management.

A coaching session is as much about mastering the conversation with the client as about being in control of your internal dialogue. In a session the coach needs to be listening at the global level. Information is captured not only from listening to what is being said and not being said, but from observation and intuition. If your self-talk is active (thinking of the next question to ask, noticing what the client is wearing, listening to music being played in the lounge, etc.), you are not paying as much attention to your client as you should. Therefore your intuition is not at full steam and that can hinder the coaching session.

When conducting a coaching session it is fundamental to reach the level of professionalism needed to excel in skills that will help the client address his own issues. Attaining full focus, full attention, control of internal dialogue and mastery of coaching skills is most likely to be achieved in a quiet environment, where you and your client feel comfortable.

In Clean Language coaching the coach asks the client to choose where he would like to sit before taking a seat. By doing this coaches show that the session is about the client, not them. The simple act of choosing a chair may be the first step toward improving the client's ability to think for themselves and learn.

13. How long should a coaching session last?

The duration of a session varies depending on the type of coaching. In life coaching a session typically lasts one hour. Executive coaching sessions tend to last between one and two hours, with the most common time frame being 90 minutes. Corporate or team coaching usually lasts all morning or afternoon, since it sometimes involves team building exercises, special meetings or other events that last longer.

Having said that, there are certain topics and exercises that can easily take over two hours, an example being value elicitation (both professional and personal). Please refer to question 49 for more details about this exercise. By contrast some sessions only last 30 minutes. It is important to emphasise that there is no relation between duration and the effectiveness of the session. Regardless of the duration, a coaching session aims to be as effective as possible.

There is another type of meeting coaches call a *consultation session*. It's nothing more than an "initial discussion" designed to draw the attention of prospects to your coaching services. The consultation sessions is free and lasts no longer than half an hour, the main objective being to get the client talking about his dilemmas and where he feels stuck. The coach then highlights how coaching can help, and what it means to work together.

Consultations aren't intended to be a free 30-minute coaching session. Otherwise the client may think that his problem is "fixed" and won't see the point of further coaching. If the topic is too big to tackle in only 30 minutes, the client may conclude that coaching is not the appropriate support needed (at least, not your services). Therefore, try to fight the temptation to coach the person during the consultation session. Focus your energy on motivating the prospect to work with you in the future.

During the time scheduled with your client it is your responsibility to manage the time properly. Managing a coaching session is not an easy task. Between being fully focused on the client and his agenda, the coach ought to take in consideration the goal set at the beginning and how to achieve a successful outcome. Therefore time management throughout the session is paramount. The last thing both client and coach want to do is to waste time. This could possibly mean more expense for the client and diary conflicts for the coach. It is the responsibility of the coach to avoid these situations.

14. How long should a coaching engagement last?

There is no precise answer to this question. A coaching engagement is a series of sessions between a coach and a client. Depending on the client's goals, the length varies.

Typically, in a triangular relationship, the sponsor expects results within a four to six month period. Therefore, in these kinds of contracts sessions can be scheduled on a weekly basis, every second week, monthly or whatever is best for clients and the fulfilment of their goal(s).

A related question is when to terminate an engagement that has already fulfilled its purpose, or a relationship in which the coach believes the client is no longer benefitting from coaching and requires a different type of support. In these cases the coach must bring the topic forward and discuss it with an open mind, ensuring the client understands the danger of proceeding with an engagement that is no longer healing or beneficial. Please read more on question 66.

However, nothing need stop the same two people from taking part in future coaching engagements. Therefore you can have several sequential (or not) engagements with the same client.

Coaching relationships will always exist. Nurturing these relationships is not an easy task, but not impossible. There is more about this subject in answer 65.

When you have several coaching engagements with the same client the relationship may mirror a good friendship. Be wary of your ability to remain challenging. Keep asking powerful questions and help the client see the issue from different angles before deciding what to do next. If necessary consult a supervisor to help you assess your objectivity. Above all remain professional, non-judgmental, and non-directive at all times.

There are some coaching relationships that begin 'pro-bono', meaning the coach offers one or more complimentary coaching sessions to a client. There are several instances when pro-bono is a well thought out approach:

- When a new coach begins his practice and must hone his skill;
- When the client lacks the financial resources to pay for services;
- When the client is a relative or friend of the coach;
- Charity;
- Personal choice of the coach.

Nevertheless the same concerns apply to a pro-bono relationship. When sessions continue after the goal has been reached it can adversely affect a professional reputation.

15. How important is a coaching code of ethics?

Although the coaching industry is in some areas its infancy and not yet fully regulated, professional coaching services ought to meet the highest standards and follow an appropriate code of conduct defined by the core values and ethics of the profession.

Any coaching practice should state clearly what its abiding ethical principles are. These are much more than a list of do's and don'ts. They include guidelines on confidentiality, management of information, hypothetical situations and practical solutions. They raise awareness on seeking continuous professional development and ensure the highest professionalism in conducting coaching sessions.

It is important for both the client and the coach to understand the boundaries, 'forbidden territories' and standards that shape the coaching relationship. Code of conduct documentation must be written in such a way that misinterpretations and/or misconceptions are avoided. This document is to be made available on request to clients and any others doing business with the coaching practice.

Failure to comply with the code of ethics may lead to disciplinary action if you are a member of a coaching school or professional body. In the worst cases it could lead to termination of membership with the coaching body and/or to legal repercussions. All coaches are advised to acquire professional indemnity insurance. This covers any situation where you may be accused of malpractice, errors, and omissions. Some liability insurance policies also cover public and product liability, libel, and slander.

The code of ethics below is my own set of coaching practice ethics and it is the result of careful research on standards and codes of conduct and ethics from various coaching bodies and from several training institutions and business consultancy service providers, such as the AC, ICF, AoEC, NMC and PwC.

Code of Ethics

All staff, tutors, associate members and colleagues of the coaching practice agree to uphold the following code of ethics and coaching standards:

Coaching Relationship

1. All members shall treat clients, colleagues and others with whom they conduct business with respect, dignity, fairness and courtesy - respecting their values, beliefs and goals (which may differ from the coach's own) and being aware of cultural, regional and linguistic differences;

2. Coaches must ensure the client fully understands the commercial coaching agreement and its terms and conditions (costs, process, location and frequency) at the beginning of the coaching relationship;

3. It is the responsibility of a coach to withdraw from practice if their ability to serve the client is diminished by illness, conflict of interest and/or any other circumstances. When coaching minors it is the responsibility of the coach to ensure they have parental permission and an adult must be present during the coaching sessions;

4. Coaches always operate within the limits of their own competence, recognising where that competence may be exceeded and, when required, referring the client to a more experienced coach or providing them with support in seeking help from a therapist, counsellor, psychiatrist or other professional advisor;

5. Coaches will not exploit their clients' trust in order to obtain sexual, emotional, financial, mental, professional benefits and/or any other benefits;

6. Coaches will respect the client's right to cease coaching at any point during the process. Coaches will not protract a coaching relationship beyond its useful life, but will encourage the client to make a change when the client is no longer benefiting from the client - coach relationship.

Confidentiality/Management of Information

1. Coaches respect the confidentiality and privacy of their clients, colleagues and others with whom they do business. Unless authorised, coaches do not use confidential information for personal use or the benefit of any third party. Coaches can disclose confidential information or personal data only when appropriate approval has been obtained and/or they are compelled to do so by legal, regulatory or professional requirements;

2. Coaches will refrain from giving professional information or advice and from making claims they know to be confidential, misleading or beyond their capacity to evaluate.

3. All members will respect copyright agreements, intellectual property and trademarks, and will comply with any regulations in these areas. Coaches shall not plagiarise another professional's work.

Professional Conduct

1. All members must conduct themselves with the highest level of ethics, integrity, accountability and responsibility to maintain the good reputation of the coaching profession and to avoid any disrepute with professional bodies and/or individual coaches;

2. Coaches should avoid any conflict of interest within the coaching relationship. However if a situation occurs that may create conflict, generate litigation or lead to negative exposure in relation to the coaching practice, the coach must take immediate action and;

   - Discuss it with the client;
   - Consult senior coaches;
   - Inform regulated coaching bodies regarding the situation.

3. All coaches will regularly participate in appropriate personal and professional development to stay up to date with new advances within the coaching industry and to enhance their skills and level of competence;

4. Coaches must have professional indemnity insurance to cover their coaching services;

5. All promotional materials and advertisements (both verbal and written) created for the coaching practice shall be legal, decent, truthful, honest, and shall comply with the legislation requirements of the country where issued;

6. Coaching must abide by all the laws and regulations of the country of the coaching practice, where coaching takes place and where the client is located;

7. Any breach of these coaching standards and code of ethics may result in disciplinary action and possibly termination of membership by the regulated coaching bodies. It may have a negative impact on the coaching image and reputation of the coaching business.

16. How do you treat confidentiality within a coaching context?

Confidentiality describes the process which assures information is accessible only by authorised individuals and that this information is protected during its lifecycle. This is important, especially within the context of coaching, because the functions of confidentiality dictate how much and which type of personal information or data can be disclosed without consent. When your coaching client feels safe that his or her information and the topics discussed during coaching sessions are kept confidential, he or she will feel more secure and will view you as the trustworthy practitioner you are.

Any information your client reveals to you should remain confidential, unless legal and/or professional requirements interfere with disclosure.

The assurance of confidentiality should be included in every coaching contract and agreement. Even if it seems repetitive, stating it will demonstrate your professionalism and the good quality standards by which you abide.

Without the client's permission you can still refer to your sessions when speaking confidentially with other coaches, during supervision, throughout examination and training courses or in other scenarios related to professional development. Of course, you must refrain from revealing the client's identity. Always strive for the highest standards of professionalism and quality in the profession, not to simply build up appearances but to build up your own reputation.

17. Why is accreditation useful?

Accreditation is the process of becoming recognised in a certain field as a valid and knowledgeable practitioner. In a self-regulated industry accreditation assures clients that you have taken the extra steps to confirm your credibility, even though you are not required to do so. Nowadays, more and more companies demand that coaching practitioners have accreditation credentials as a way of safeguarding the company's image and avoiding any unpleasant business situations.

In addition, the bodies that provide accreditation also create industry standards and influence the code of ethics across the industry. Therefore accreditation can vouch for the coach's competence, skill and knowledge.

In promotional material or verbal communication a coach affirms he or she is accredited and his or her credibility rises tremendously.

Several international bodies[2] provide accreditation procedures, including:

- **International Coaching Federation – ICF** – An American institution incorporating several dozen groups called ICF Chapters in over 90 countries;
- **Association for Coaching – AC** – A global association with headquarters in the UK. It regulates industry standards and is a good platform for continuous development;
- **International Institute of Coaching – IIC** – The former European Coaching Institute (ECI), which has expanded to 75 countries. IIC is managed by a volunteer group of coaches;
- **European Mentoring & Coaching Council** – Provides course and individual accreditation at four levels across Europe.

Several coaching schools, such as The Academy of Executive Coaching, have a thorough evaluation process, and provide an accreditation certificate at graduation. The coach needs to follow a re-accreditation process after one year and then every three years, in order to maintain standards and credibility.

Accreditation isn't synonymous with membership. However, one can become member of these bodies without being accredited by them. For both accreditation and membership a reasonable fee is paid. Accreditation requires an administration fee. Membership fees are the cost for benefits which may include: access to forums, notice boards, mastermind classes, workshop attendance at special prices, coaching supervision and a webpage profile visible to potential corporate clients.

---

2. Refer to Appendix I for contact details for these professional bodies.

In order to get through accreditation the requirements are much more than an administration fee. Besides oral examination and written assignments, the coach needs to show evidence of coaching hours, training programmes attendance, testimonials from paying clients, letters of references from qualified and accredited coaches, proof of further CPD and any articles written or workshops facilitated by the applicant. Some accreditation requires supervision or 'mentor coaching'. The accreditation process can take months to complete, but it is definitely worthwhile pursuing it.

There are many other organisations and institutions that will certify you in the coaching profession. Always associate yourself with a respected and valid authority in the accreditation field.

Although accreditation is a step closer to higher credibility, your own professionalism and the way clients perceive you is most important. The combination of accreditation and professionalism will undoubtedly result in a powerful outcome.

18. Who dictates the coaching industry standards?

The coaching standards for the entire industry are dictated by the same bodies providing accreditation to coaches. Please refer to question 17 for a list of the most prominent global bodies in the coaching industry. There are also many other local and international organisations.

Their mission is to establish coaching ethics, define excellence for the industry, promote best practices in coaching and raise awareness. All of these organisations have been pro-actively surveying the coaching world on a number of topics in order to better define coaching standards and to create certain rules coaches must follow. A new member of these associations signs their declaration of integrity and is bound by their code of ethics, good practice policies, privacy rules and data protection guidelines.

These organisations have elected global boards and representative delegations on a country level. The country representatives oversee the institution locally. Initially individual delegates may be appointed by the boards and subsequently are elected by popular vote.

I strongly recommend checking out their websites as they provide loads of information about various topics. They are a good starting point if you would like to learn more about regulation in the industry.

It is worth contacting the coaching organisations in your country. A significant amount of smaller local bodies regulate the coaching industry by considering certain legalities and local laws.

Last but not least, each of the national or global bodies usually organises an annual general assembly or conference. Members and non-members are welcome. These bring together like-minded people interested in coaching, brainstorming, developing subjects, debating certain issues and bridging relationships between attendees. This is certainly a good way to increase your network and create business partnerships.

For more information on these events check their websites.

19. What should be included in a coaching contract?

The coaching contract is a document which stipulates the agreement between the parties involved in an engagement, whether it is a dual (client – coach) or a triangular relationship (coach – client – sponsor).

Essential contract elements include:

- Names of the parties involved;
- Goals and objectives for the coaching engagement;
- Confidentiality agreement;
- Length of contract;
- Fees and invoicing;
- Other expenses (such as travelling, accommodation, mileage, etc.);
- Frequency and duration of coaching sessions;
- Where coaching sessions will take place;
- Progress and final reports;
- Beginning and review meetings with all parties involved;
- Measure of success;
- ROI calculation method;
- Your coaching model (optional);
- Cancellation policy;
- Boundaries (other types of support, such as mentoring, counselling, etc.);
- Termination clause;
- Breach procedures;
- Evaluation and feedback process;
- Request for references and testimonials.

Terms & Conditions, detailed explanations of procedures and the code of ethics followed by your practice are documents made available as appendices to the contract. Note that the terms and conditions, as well as the code of ethics, remain standard documents independent of the contract. The contract is the only document that may change.

Whilst it is important to have written contracts, especially if you operate a limited company, they are often based on spoken terms. It is always advisable to follow-up with a short email or written communication to confirm the agreed terms.

The termination clause is helpful not only for the client but also for the coach. Basically, the clause says that at any given time the client or coach can cease the engagement, regardless of the reason. It is not common for a coach to cease an engagement with a client and the main reasons for doing so often stem from the coach's own 'forbidden territories' and value system conflicts with the client.

Regarding 'forbidden territories' there may be certain topics personal to the coach that make it difficult for the coach to feel they can stay objective and in integrity by working with the client. In such situations it is recommended that the coach consults with a supervisor to think through the best approach. For further reading please refer to question 50.

With regards to conflicting value systems, discuss this with your supervisor as well, although in this case he may not add much more than just, "Follow your heart".

Other possible reasons for terminating a coaching contract are discussed in the answer to question 66.

20. What is the best policy for managing last minute cancellations?

Generally speaking any type of cancellation is an annoyance for both the receiver and the one requesting the cancellation. The coach must fill this time slot with something else. The client may now have added concerns and stresses linked with having the coaching session cancelled.

Cancellations, as well as other ground rules and ethics, should be explicitly stated in the contract agreement whether the client is an individual or a corporate employer.

Note that cancellations can be requested by both the client and the coach, regardless of the reason. Nevertheless, any cancellation policy has to be communicated to the client, both verbally and in writing, in order to avoid misunderstandings.

Some coaching businesses distinguish between different types of cancellation notices. Some coaches require payment for same-day cancellations. However, if cancellation is requested the day before the client pays only 50% of the session's value. If cancelled 48 hours in advance, the coaching session is rescheduled at no extra cost.

While caring for the client is important to every coach, coaches are in business and have financial obligations as well. The old maxim, *Time is money,* applies.

The best policy for cancellations must resonate with you as a coach and human being, and the way you conduct your coaching business. However, don't make procedures so strict that your clients will want to work with a competitor in the future.

My recommendation is to create fair rules and stick to them. If you are really adding value to a client's life he or she will think twice before cancelling and will understand, and follow, the policy.

21. How much should coaches charge for coaching sessions?

Coaching rates vary and are impacted by several factors:

- Target audience;
- Product;
- Accreditation and qualifications;
- Experience;
- Location;
- Competition;
- Your mindset.

First, identify your target audience. Different rates apply for a senior manager of a global company or a housewife in your neighbourhood. Some coaches have different rates for different customer clusters, even though the products or services they offer are reasonably similar.

Second, clearly state your services. Is it executive coaching, life coaching or business coaching? A product or a service can also be sold as a part of a package. This package can be linked with promotions, such as "buy four sessions and get the fifth free" that impact the cost of a unit.

If you have completed rigorous qualifications and extensive accreditation processes with well-known and respected training and accreditation bodies, it is acceptable to increase your prices accordingly. Nevertheless, the experience you already have under your belt is fundamental to determining your starting price. It is not uncommon to see junior coaches charging as much as their supervisors or senior coaches. Your fees must be balanced according to the factors mentioned above.

The established location of your coaching practice is less relevant for the monetary equation than the location of your sessions. All the expenses you incur (transport, mileage, accommodation, etc.) add to the cost of the coaching session, unless it is included in a package or you have a special deal with a particular client.

Finally, your fees must mirror those of your competition. If you charge much less than the competition or the industry standard your clients will question the real value of your services. Despite the fact that you offer skills and support to help the client move forward in society value almost always equals price.

On the other hand, if your price is too high, potential clients will shop around for more reasonably priced services. The main difference between you and your competitors is the bond you create with your clients. Hopefully, it will be better than the bond your competitor creates with clients. It is very subjective, but aren't all relationships a bit subjective?

Last but not least, your rate depends on your mindset. Your confidence and belief in your ability to help others will attract clients. Charge what you think you are worth, but tempered by these other factors we have discussed. Be congruent with your values. Above all, be honest with yourself about your limitations and potential.

At the time this book went to print, the executive coaching rates in major cities such as London started at £350 for a 90 to 120-minute coaching session sponsored by the employer. For privately arranged coaching, the fees vary between £100 and £150 for 60-minute sessions. These prices can include packages with unlimited email support, 24-hr response rate, post-meeting call support, etc.

According to life coaches working in the main urban areas, fees vary from £50 to £150.

22. What is coaching supervision?

Coaching supervision is a continuous improvement tool that all coaches should use in order to clarify doubts, to get honest feedback about their skills and to improve their practice.

A supervisor acts as a sounding board for the practitioner. His or her doubts and fears, questions and uncertainties can be managed by the supervisor, who should be a very experienced and knowledgeable coach acting as a mentor and offering an opinion on specific issues. Typically, a supervisor could help the coach on the following points:

- 'How should I act in a given situation?'
- 'What could I do/have done in this situation?'
- 'What skills could have helped in that moment?'

Note that the issue does not necessarily have to be in the past. It can be a future situation. Topics such as self-management, 'forbidden territories' for the coach and uncertainties are good matters to discuss with your supervisor, who is expected to be a senior master coach with hundreds of coaching hours under his belt. As they say, *"In doubt, consult"*.

Supervision can take place 'live', when the supervisor joins the coaching session to assess the coach's skills and overall practice. The supervisor's feedback and evaluation of the session is an essential part of the coach's continuous improvement. Here supervisor and coach discuss the details and more adequate methods, tools and skills are highlighted. Then the coach is better prepared to approach the situation with greater professionalism next time. No two coaching sessions are the same, so the coach must assess and use his best judgement in deciding when to apply what he has discussed with his supervisor.

Interestingly, there are some accreditation bodies that require the coach to participate in several hours of supervision to become accredited, which they refer to as 'mentor coaching'. Supervision can also be handled as a group call, with the supervision rate being split between the coaches being supervised.

Moreover, the supervisor has a 'duty of care' to the end user, the coachee, and is liable to the professional body or court of law for the conduct of the coach. Supervision is, without doubt, an essential component of the practice and all coaches should at some point in their careers have a supervisor.

On another note, it is important to make the distinction between supervising a coach and coaching a coach. As you probably know by now, a coach also needs to be coached through his or her own problems and dilemmas as a human being, a professional, a spouse and so on. Normally the topics raised in a supervision session are different from those in a regular coaching session. The supervisor is expected to give his opinion and advice, which is not the case in a regular coaching session.

A supervision session, like a coaching session, can take place over the phone, over the Internet or in a face-to-face meeting. The venue depends on both supervisor and coach. On this note, when supervision takes the form of being present in a coaching session to witness the way the coach handles a session with his client, it is critical to get the client's permission for the supervisor to be present prior to the session, regardless of its format (phone call, Skype, face-to-face meeting).

To summarise, the benefits a coach receives from supervision are in his own continuous improvement as a professional coach and in the development of his business.

23. Where can coaching supervision be found?

Coaching supervision is not difficult to find. Basically, you need a more experienced qualified coach willing to supervise your coaching sessions and clarify your doubts.

To find a suitable supervisor:

- Browse your coaching association membership websites and post a note about supervision;
- Approach a coach directly and make him/her a proposal about supervision;
- Mention it in your local coaches' support group;
- Talk to previous tutors and facilitators of your coaching courses;
- Write and ask authors of coaching books;
- Contact accreditation bodies.

Wherever you choose to find a supervising coach, it's important to select a supervisor based upon:

- Supervisor's experience;
- Supervisor's qualifications;
- Trust and honesty.

For you to benefit, the supervising coach needs to be more experienced and definitely a qualified and accredited coach. He or she doesn't need to be older, even though age is often synonymous with experience.

Some accreditation bodies require the applicant to be supervised for a certain number of hours before granting accreditation. The supervisor may have to be someone already accredited by that institution, as in the case of ICF accreditation. Many coaches are willing to provide group supervision at discount rates or even pro-bono supervision by request.

Finally, as in any coaching relationship, good supervision is based on authentic trust and honesty. The coach needs to feel safe regarding certain subjects and supported in dealing positively with feedback. Not all feedback is going to be positive and affirming.

The aim of supervision is to point out aspects of coaching needing further development and improvement. Therefore, don't take feedback personally and be open to trying new methods. After all, supervision is only effective when the receiver decides to act upon the information given and is willing to stretch his own comfort zone to prepare for different situations.

In group supervision confidentiality is essential as well as a willingness to open up to someone other than your supervisor. Despite the fact that you will learn from someone else's problems, the most important goal is your own progress and evolution as a professional. If that means you prefer individual coaching supervision, so be it!

Even though accreditation of supervisors is not common yet, accreditation bodies such as the EMCC and the AC require some sort of qualification or endorsement of experience for supervisors.

Most certainly in a few years supervisors will have to be accredited – in fact the APECS (Association of Professional Executive Coaches & Supervisors) already accredits supervisors.

24. Why should a coach be coached?

For the reasons why a coach needs to be coached look at the reasons why anyone might need coaching. A coach also benefits from being challenged in a safe environment, breaking old thinking patterns that aren't helpful and having non-judgmental, non-directive support for structuring his thinking and planning.

A coach can draw from the experience of being a client and can use exercises practised during the sessions. He or she can adapt other tools and methodologies learned while being coached.

Coaching a coach is different from supervising a coach. The topics brought up by a coach during a session are personal or professional as if he were any other client.

Choosing a coach is an interesting task. Some coaches prefer someone with a different approach, so they can learn more about themselves. Others get more out of coaching of a similar style to their own, so they can fully embark on the journey of self-discovery. Either way, it's important for the coach as client to fully benefit from the sessions and to reach predetermined goals, instead of simply trying to learn new tricks. For this reason coaching a coach is not an easy task. The coach as client could quickly derail the sessions and begin judging or evaluating the practitioner's approach. Of course it also happens with clients in other professions, such as law and medicine, when they require the services of a colleague. It is natural to assess skills and judge conclusions.

The relationship between coach and coach-client needs to be based on trust and honesty, while the coach abides by a code of ethics that honours confidentiality and other aspects of information management.

Some coaches develop a unique relationship and coach one another. With a very close relationship this works well, if both parties remain impartial and non-judgmental throughout the engagement.

25. How do referrals work?

A referral is a recommendation from a client, a friend or even another coach or practitioner.

Normally, your good work speaks for itself and colleagues are more than willing to recommend you to their friends and acquaintances. You only need to do a good job.

Why would another coach refer clients to you? Certainly he or she would enjoy that source of income themselves. True. But it's not that simple. Some reasons to refer clients to another practitioner are:

- Different specialisations;
- Too many active clients;
- Lack of rapport with a specific client;
- Decision not to coach family members or friends;
- Self-defined boundaries.

Coaching has different niches and specialisations. If you are an executive coach and someone requires an adolescence coach, you will happily refer to colleagues who are more skilled in those areas.

Even though building rapport with your client is a coaching skill, you are human. Sometimes a coach and client don't click. In these cases it is better to be honest and a referral is in the best interests of the client.

Some coaches are adamantly opposed to coaching their relatives and circle of friends. They feel that if they are too close to the person they cannot remain impartial during the session. They may begin advising and counselling rather than coaching. Personally I understand this point of view. However, some coaches are able to distance themselves and refrain from presenting opinions and judgements.

Self-management is a very important topic for a coach as it requires deep honesty about what makes you uncomfortable. For instance a pro-birth coach, who naturally disagrees with abortion, may be partial when her client talks about getting an abortion. While some coaches master impartiality and the acceptance of different points of view, others don't. In those cases, a referral to another competent practitioner is essential. Self-management is a good topic to discuss with your supervisor. It is essential to be part of a good network of coaches. Despite the fact that other coaches are your competitors, they are also potential allies.

The last point I would like to highlight regarding referrals is the dynamics. Many coaches receive a commission for each referral they provide to colleagues. The fee varies from 10% to 100% of the first coaching session. After the first meeting the relationship is between the client and new coach and the referrer has no further say.

Some coaches promote their services by offering a free session to existing clients who recommend their services to friends and acquaintances, who in turn become paying clients.

The rules you define for your practice have to be fair, to resonate with you and to comply with industry standards.

26. What is the impact of a testimonial?

A positive testimonial can do wonders for your practice. Testimonials are simply comments about you as a coach, your skills and how clients felt you helped them find solutions to their problems. A genuine and sincere testimonial can influence an undecided potential client.

Testimonials don't necessarily come from previous or current clients. A tribute from someone recognised and famous in the industry is always nice and can be another positive influence on the prospect. Famous people in the industry tend to be presidents or members of the board of associations or institutions related to coaching or authors of well-known coaching book.

Regardless of who writes the testimonial, the important prerequisite is knowing you, having experienced your coaching personally, supervised you or shared in co-coaching.

You need to carefully select the testimonials for the best impact on the reader before sharing them with the public. Obviously, you won't share a testimonial regarding your weaknesses. In addition, some testimonials are ambivalent. Beware of these comments, for they are potentially harmful. Be absolutely happy with what is written and certain that there won't be misinterpretations, before publication.

In addition, the author must give permission for publication. As a professional you must solicit agreement before publishing a testimonial on your website and/or promotional material. Some people agree on the condition that their full name is kept secret. Being clear upfront will prevent future problems. Key testimonials build up your credibility, especially if they identify the employers and job titles of the person giving the testimonial.

Some testimonials are so juicy with their praise about your skills that they sound too good to be true. At some point they become pointless, almost like those one-sentence book or film reviews written on a back cover or a promotional poster that say things like *"A must!"* or *"Incredibly talented!"*

Prospects are looking for authentic and genuine feedback about your coaching skills, not unnatural exaggerations that push them away.

Testimonials should be sharp and to the point. A lengthy comment will bore your prospect and convey your coaching style falsely. Make sure they aren't egocentric, long or uninteresting. Two or three sentences, maximum, will do the job nicely.

Last but not least, be as diverse as possible in selecting testimonials - different age groups, genders, professions, etc. Testimonials from relatives (people with the same surname) may send the wrong signal. Remember that testimonials are like bridges you build to create a bond with your prospect, who will, hopefully, become your client. The bridges must be strong, straightforward and safe.

27. When should I pursue further development in my coaching career?

In the coaching industry new tools and methodologies are constantly developing. Your toolbox should be evolving and be continually updated in order for you to use the most effective processes, techniques and exercises during your coaching sessions.

With this in mind the answer to the question is simple: every day is a good time to pursue further development. Some accreditation bodies request annual proof of participation in coaching courses, workshops, seminars, etc. A specific number of training and coaching hours are required.

Explore the coaching world. Many existing approaches can improve your current practice. These include:

- Psychological methodologies, e.g. NLP[3], Gestalt, Cognitive Behavioural Coaching, Transactional Analysis, Somatic/Body Work;
- Creative Arts – use of voice, drawing, movement, story telling;
- Clean Language - the exploration and use of the clients' metaphors;
- The healing energy of Reiki and its importance in spiritual coaching;
- EFT[4];
- Refreshing your skills with an advanced coaching course;
- Learning new skills such as speaking to big audiences;
- Meditation;
- Specialising in another area of coaching.

The list of possibilities is vast and it may be difficult to decide which programme to pick first.

Another important topic to emphasise is the potential loneliness of the coaching profession. It is easy to become isolated. If you qualified through a distant learning process, consider taking a course based on face-to-face meetings. Take advantage of mingling with people, increasing your network and improving interpersonal skills. Networking will certainly be a very good addition to your toolbox.

---

3. NLP – Neuro Linguistic Programming.
4. EFL – Emotional Freedom Technique is a form of psychological acupressure. It applies the energy meridians used in traditional acupuncture, but without needles. According to Gary Craig, a recognised voice in the field, *"EFT is an emotional version of acupuncture wherein we stimulate certain meridian points by tapping on them with our fingertips. Properly done, this frequently reduces the therapeutic process from months or years down to hours or minutes. And, since emotional stress can contribute to pain, disease and physical ailments, we often find that EFT provides astonishing physical relief."*

My advice is choosing the course providing the fastest and most effective results in your coaching and individual development. Follow your intuition and step into one of these fields.

Don't forget to keep your certificate of attendance and completion handy, as evidence of your effort.

28. How do I know which coaching books to read?

There are several different ways to choose the next book to read. It's less about picking the best and more about choosing one that speaks to you. Below are simple ways to search for enlightening books:

1. **Look at the most popular books online**
   Amazon.com is the most popular online book seller. Thousands of people buy books through Amazon for convenience and for further reading recommendations. Their *'other readers also buy ABC book'* section and the list of most popular books are good features. It is worthwhile spending a few moments browsing through these two lists as they offer good suggestions. Amazon has added a special feature for some books which enables you to view inside the first pages of the book, including the table of contents, to give you a good idea of the content and style;

2. **Check reader's reviews**
   Book reviews are another source of suggestions highlighting subjects and perspectives. Nowadays book reviews aren't limited to paper magazines. You can easily find book reviews in electronic bulletins from coaching associations, e-zines and online booksellers. Take time to read some of the reviews. You may find interesting ideas to help you decide on your next read;

3. **Recommended reading list from your coaching course**
   Your coaching course most definitely has a list of recommended reading to deepen your knowledge on current teachings and broaden your education. Make sure you are aware of this list by talking to your tutors;

4. **Ask your coaching colleagues for their reading suggestions**
   Your coaching network is another source of information for books of interest. Ask your colleagues what they would recommend;

5. **Browse the websites of coaching organisations**
   The majority of coaching organisations have a section entitled *Reading* or *Bookstore* on their websites. The objective is to sell books online, but just skim the lists for ideas. Then you can buy via their site or copy the information and purchase the material from a preferred seller;

6. **Browse the internet or bookstore**

Even though it is a more intuitive approach, browsing is practised by a large number of people. It is skimming through books, letting the book *talk* to them either through the cover design, the words on the back cover, the table of contents, the introduction, or the name and picture of the author. There isn't any specific science to it. You make your decision based on the energy you receive from the bits of information you have about the book, on the spot. Either you like it, or you don't.

I have personally used all of these options to find excellent suggestions and great books. Most importantly the decision to buy the book is yours. It is not simply because a colleague says it is good. Follow your intuition and I am sure you will not regret it!

29. How is the benefit-cost ratio calculated?

The clearest explanation of Return on Investment (ROI) within the coaching world and how to calculate the benefit-cost ratio are described by Mary Beth O'Neil in her book *Executive Coaching with Backbone and Heart.* The author explains the importance of requesting quantifiable and tangible goals from the client, in order to facilitate the process of ROI calculation later on in the process.

The formula used for the benefit-cost ratio is:

$$\frac{\text{Business results x \% of coaching impact}}{\text{Cost of the investment}}$$

In this equation, the three components require careful thought. Business results are linked to department achievements after coaching the director. Select the numbers carefully since they impact the return on investment. A higher business result number will not necessarily mean a higher return on investment since other components change.

The percentage of coaching impact is assessed by the client after weighing all variables contributing to the outcome. The variables may include:

- Team building exercises;
- Bonuses and incentives;
- Different reports;
- Management tools.

Normally the client tends to attribute a higher weight to the impact of coaching. It's important that your client is frank about the true value of the coaching, doesn't play the nice customer role and is realistic and businesslike.

The cost of the investment is basically the fees for your coaching services including expenses incurred while provide your services, such as travelling and accommodation. According to Mary Beth O'Neil *"the impact executive coaching has had on bottom-line results averages between 15 and 33%".*

The ROI calculation is often the basis of a stronger marketing strategy for any business. Showing the new prospect managerial evidence that your services have approximately a 33% impact on business growth for other clients is irrefutable proof that your coaching is a worthwhile investment.

I suggest that you read Mary Beth's book, and others on ROI and the benefit-cost ratio application in the coaching world.

30. How can behavioural improvements be assessed?

Individuals and companies find coaching useful for improving business results and helping managers climb the career ladder to higher positions in the organisation. Coaching supports them through change, conflict resolution, leadership skills improvement, etc. A substantial part of coaching is required for behavioural enhancement.

Business results are tangible, quantifiable and measurable, and they can always be improved. The old management maxim says *"If you can measure it, you can improve it"*. It's relatively easy to assess the improvement of something measurable.

However, when it comes to improving behaviour it gets trickier since it's subjective. A seemingly acceptable behaviour falls short of someone else's expectations.

Assess behavioural improvement objectively, use plenty of intuition and be sincere. A form listing ideal behaviours is a good tool. Include a one to ten scale assessing the client before coaching starts and again at the end of the contracted period. The form is completed by the client and, in a triangular relationship, by his or her sponsor. It is helpful to specify these behaviours and actions so that they can easily be observed. Therefore answering the following questions helps the assessment process:

- What triggered this behaviour?
- How many times did it happen?
- How well was it demonstrated?
- What components of the behaviour were shown?
- What other components need to be demonstrated?

When possible, request specific examples of the behaviour(s) to be demonstrated and the actions to be implemented.

As the coaching engagement progresses, ask your client and the evaluator(s) to re-assess and identify any changes. Repeat the same procedure once the coaching engagement is concluded.

With each form you have the opportunity to question the sincerity of the answers provided by both the individual and evaluators. Your intuition plays an important role and you ought to express it often. Don't be worried about wrong hunches. The client will let you know. When it comes to intuition it isn't the interpretation itself that counts but the client's response and making him reflect.

Encourage the client see that he or she is a winner when being authentic, honest and sincere. It makes the process more fruitful for everyone.

31. Why is evaluation of a coaching engagement necessary?

Evaluation of the coaching engagement is an important step, both when contracting directly with the individual or in a triangular relationship. The topic is raised up-front so that the client knows what is expected when the engagement comes to an end.

Any type of feedback is a gift. It provides you with a list of possible improvements. Feedback is an invitation to learn from every client experience. It gives you an idea of how to improve in the future.

When receiving feedback from a client:

1. **Check your understanding** – if you are confused, ask for clarification. Taking a few moments to understand will allow your emotional charge to reduce;

2. **Deal with your feelings** – Be prepared to accept some pain when dealing with feedback;

3. **Look for the lesson** – When the emotional charge is controlled and you have dealt with your feelings think about the value of the feedback and ask yourself what you could do differently next time;

4. **Don't fight the feedback** – Try to separate the content of the feedback from the source.

You, as a coach more than anyone, should accept the feedback in a professional manner, looking for the lessons.

Have an evaluation form prepared for clients for when the engagement is finished. During the sessions when your client feels closer to you, his opinion of you may be inflated and affect the final scores. In the pursuit of results that reflect the true opinions of clients, coaches should request feedback only after the coaching relationship is finished.

The template should have quantifying questions for evaluating skills such as rapport, empathy, active listening and questioning. Include a simple scale from one to ten, (ten being the highest) to make it easy for the client. In addition have a section in the template where the client can give more elaborated answers and specific feedback. Below are a few examples of questions:

- How would you describe the coaching relationship?
- What additional support would you have appreciated from your coach?
- What specifically did you appreciate about your coach?
- On which occasions would you have liked to be more, or less, challenged?

- What could have improved your journey/coaching engagement?
- What specific advice could you give for improving the coach's practice?
- What specifically would you like to have tried during the coaching engagement?

Ideally, the feedback should be written and recorded but if there is no time for that you can request that the client uses voice messaging or other auditory technology.

It is important to finish a coaching relationship on a positive note. You never know when you will do business with the same person or what the potential impact of their referrals might be. That's why it is important to accept feedback in a professional manner. Thank your client for his or her time in completing the evaluation form. Take their opinions seriously and set goals for improving your skills. Try incorporating some of their suggestions in your day-in-day-out practice.

32. What restrictions are there regarding coaching family members and friends?

There aren't any written rules about coaching relatives and friends (unlike in counselling and therapy). The decision is entirely up to you. Although it remains a personal choice, it is interesting to highlight advantages and disadvantages:

Advantages

- You already have a trustworthy and honest relationship;
- You are already aware of events and situations in that person's life;
- They know your values and your beliefs, and you know theirs;
- Marketing and selling efforts are reduced to the minimum;
- A sense of support is shared. The client feels he or she is giving the coach some support, if only monetary.

Disadvantages

- Even though the relationship is good, it may not be open enough in a coaching environment;
- You may have misconceptions about certain events and situations in that person's past and have already formulated some opinions;
- It may be difficult to get them to try new things or break old thinking patterns;
- It's tempting to jump into advice mode and to share your opinions on 'fixing the problem';
- You may feel uncomfortable charging your family members and friends for services
- Your coaching may become judgmental and directional;
- The coachee may misinterpret your exercises, methodologies or questions and this may harm your friendship/relationship;
- The coachee may feel the relationship/friendship is unbalanced in coaching and start feeling inferior;
- Your time with your relatives and friends is only in a coaching environment. You may miss out on your former relationship/friendship.

This is not an exhaustive list. Nevertheless, if one can separate these worlds – coaching and the relationship/friendship – you can definitely become a helpful support to relatives and friends. It's important to note that not everyone is comfortable sharing a darker side with someone so close to them. In those cases you need to accept the fact and not take it personally.

Part II – Core Aspects of the Coaching Practice

The objective of this section is to clarify doubts related to practising coaching and what to have in mind when conducting a coaching session. It will shed light on some of the fears and uncertainties shared by many coaches. It answers 50 questions, includes tips and provides practical recommendations for coaching.

33. What are the most common mistakes coaches make?

Below are a few common mistakes that inexperienced coaches tend to make:

- Worrying about the next question;
- Using inadequate words;
- Communicating in one dimension;
- Answering only certain questions;
- Poor self-management;
- Giving advice and suggestions;
- Reverting to self-protection.

Aspiring and inexperienced coaches often worry about the next question for their clients. They are preoccupied and lose focus on the current conversation. It works as a self-fulfilling prophecy – "I don't know what to ask", "Should it be a 'what' or a 'how' question?" Suddenly the coach may realise the client has stopped talking and that they, the coach, missed the last part of the conversation. Don't worry about the next question. In fact, by really paying attention, the coach will have enough information to know the next question.

Some words like 'should', 'have to', 'must', 'ought to' and 'need to' are used by inexperienced coaches and should be dropped from their vocabulary. Most of the time these words suggest a direction, lead to a certain choice or cause the client to interpret them as the coach's preference and let them influence their decisions. Best practices recommend the coach replace these words with 'could' and start using more conditional tense forms rather than the future tense. For example, ask "What could you do?" instead of "What are you going to do?", "What will you do?" or "What should you do?"

The information shared during a coaching session is more than what you hear. The client also communicates through body language, silence and hesitations. In addition intuition is a great source of information. Learn to use and trust it: no doubt it will provide interesting observations about what your client is not saying.

Myles Downey in *Effective Coaching*, explains that openness is an important piece of the coaching relationship puzzle. While coaches need to be non-judgmental and non-directive, the client clearly solicits the coach's opinion on given subjects. Once in a while a client asks a question like "What do you think?" or "What do you think I should do?" The junior coach tends to answer with his or her own humble opinion. It may seem impolite not to answer a direct question, but there are subtle ways to refocus the client's attention on options previously mentioned or to elicit further new ideas.

In these situations Downey suggests the coach probes the reasons why the client wants his opinion. More often than not the client is seeking reassurance about his own conclusions, ideas and thoughts and is not specifically looking for the coach's opinion. Downey goes even further, recommending the coach turn the tables by asking the client's opinion before sharing his own. Writer Joe Armstrong is also of the opinion that the coach can simply make the client see that his opinion isn't relevant for the case.

While being non-judgmental is key for a good coaching relationship, no coaching relationship forces you to drop your own set of beliefs, values and opinions. The coach simply controls his or her opinions during a coaching session. To control thoughts and emotions, practise *clearing inner space* before a session. To read more about this, refer to the answer to question 63.

At the beginning of a coaching career, and when dealing with certain clients, a coach may be drawn into offering advice and suggestions about better, or different, ways of looking at a problem or approaching a situation. This is one of the biggest mistakes a coach can make. Certainly, in situations when the client is really stuck techniques like brainstorming or a simple "May I offer you my views?" may help. However, in the early stages of their coaching careers there are a number of cases where coaches have decided to give their own opinions or to suggest solutions to clients' problems. This is not good practice as it changes the focus from the client to the coach.

Curly Martin, in her book *The Life Coaching Handbook,* explains the importance of a coach detaching himself from the clients' problem. If the coach gets emotionally involved, particularly because he or she has experienced a similar issue, it becomes difficult to remain impartial and non-judgmental. This leads to offering advice based on personal or past experience. According to Martin this is more apparent in relationship coaching and she explicitly recommends coaches who cannot refrain from advising based on personal experiences not to specialise in relationship coaching.

Another common mistake is reverting back to one's own self-protecting agenda when coaching someone through a crisis. It is fundamental to recognise the needs of the client and not to assume what their requirements are.

Take the time to properly prepare for the coaching session. Poor self-management can lead the way to active self-talk during a client's session, to breaking concentration and attentiveness and to lapsing from active listening skills. When the coach hasn't properly prepared beforehand it is hard for them to stay focused on what the client is saying and how he is saying it. The coach may become more judgmental and directional, so losing the foundations of coaching and the ability to help clients find solutions and practise self-discovery.

34. What is the best coaching model to follow?

There isn't one best coaching model. Ask yourself why a coaching session has to follow a specific model. Many experienced coaches don't follow a single specific coaching model. They use bits and pieces of several methodologies to help the sessions flow.

Dozens of models are used. For example, process-oriented models shape the coaching into a neat, step-by-step approach. The most popular of these is the TGROW model. There are models based on a mastery of coaching skills. Other models have roots buried deep in psychology and the Gestalt theory.

The best coaching model is determined by the practitioner. He or she decides whether a specific model matches his or her coaching style, personal view of the world and how to progress in his or her practice.

Take certain factors into consideration when adopting a certain coaching model. These include:

- Flexibility versus rigidity of use;
- Ability to challenge the client to think 'outside the box' and to see a different perspective;
- Opportunity to request feedback and continuously improve;
- Sensitivity to client's style;
- Better understanding;
- No restrictions to where / how it applies.

Some process models are too rigid and force the coach to follow a certain sequence of steps. One of the advantages of the TGROW model is the flexibility to leap from phase to phase, without the need to follow a certain sequence.

As Gerard O'Donovan, President of the IIC wrote:

"A coaching model is nothing more than a series of well-developed questions created to assist your clients with getting answers...therefore, finding solutions...to their own business or personal struggles. A few simple, well placed questions can 'flip the switch', so to speak, in your client's mind. As the coach, you learn more about how your client processes information, while your client digs deeper to tackle challenges within the confines of the trusted coaching relationship.

One specific model used regularly by trained coaches is the "T-GROW' model. GROW is an acronym for 'goals', 'reality', 'options' and 'way'. Other models include the IDEAL model, the 3 R model, COADEX, The Ten Questions of Performance, the ACHIEVE coaching model, DECOADER, OSKAR, the DRIP method, and others. Coaching schools all over the world teach these models, because they are proven to be effective. Why do we need so many models? Just like a carpenter may use one type of hammer for one type of nail and another for another type of nail, these different models meet the needs of diverse clients. The client decides what they need...the coach simply reaches into his virtual toolkit to access the best solution."

Certain models help facilitate the client's view, so he can see the problem as if he were a third person. Such models guide the client to think through other perspectives and to see events from a new angle. The rewards for completing the coaching process include self-discovery and the ability to see different solutions to the same issue. Challenging the client, in a supportive way, is what coaching is all about.

Whatever model you follow in any given session, retain the ability to request feedback, so that you can continue to improve and enhance your skills. If the model doesn't allow for that, make sure to solicit feedback from the client at the end of the session. Simple questions, such as "How could I have conducted this session to help you reach a better outcome?", "What other ways would you have liked me to coach you?" or "How do you think I can enhance my coaching skills?" are questions that will trigger a genuine and authentic response.

Some models don't fit the client's needs, especially if he or she is trying to get unstuck or is looking for ways towards an achievable outcome. At times certain otherwise effective techniques will prove inadequate. For example, requesting your client to draw a picture when they aren't at all visual will not be helpful. Trust in your intuition to help assess what is best for the situation and to guide the session.

A coaching session is not the place to try to understand how a specific model unfolds and works. As a professional coach, you must master your game. Therefore, learning specific models can be done beforehand with colleagues who may become clients during your experiments. Also, discuss any model you don't clearly understand with your supervisor in order to learn and openly discuss the techniques. Different models require certain materials, such as flipcharts. An easy model is applicable anywhere, without demanding restrictions and materials.

Finally, you don't have to stick to the same model every single session - you can vary techniques and try new things. Remember to test them in a safe environment first and only then use them with paying clients. Stretching your comfort zone will help to accelerate your learning process and comfort level, helping you grow into an excellent coach.

Learning to let go of a specific structure is one of the main differences between junior and experienced coaches. The latter feel more comfortable dancing in the moment and following their intuition, while aspiring coaches tend to rely on step-by-step coaching models as they build confidence in their skills.

As you evolve in your coaching journey you will naturally stop relying on a specific model and use a more skills-based approach, trusting your instincts more each day.

35. Must all coaching sessions begin with goal setting?

The simple answer is no. In fact, several coaches don't follow a step-by-step approach in their sessions and don't ask about specific goals at the beginning of a session. It can be very effective to clarify what the clients objectives are at the beginning of the session. This also allows you to measure whether you have been effective in following the client's needs. One powerful question to ask at the beginning is, "If this coaching session is successful, what will you have achieved?"

As you learn more about coaching and practise techniques you will find tremendous value in letting go of a step-by-step model that starts with goal setting. You can be guided by intuition and curiosity, exploring the information provided from all your senses (visual, auditory, intuitive...).

When constructing your own coaching model think about what best resonates with you. Do you like following a simple well-thought out process or do you go with the flow? Are you more interested in exploring feelings or do you prefer to focus on actions and steps?

It is important to learn how your client processes information so that you can help him to make relevant breakthroughs in his journey. If the client is a process-focused manager probably a step-by-step approach is relevant, as well as starting with goal setting. However, if the client is a creative artist, using pictures and shapes may result in a better outcome than just talking.

Again, coaching is about the client - understanding him and the way he expresses his feelings, fears and beliefs. Adapt your approach to the person in front of you and select the best tools for enabling self-discovery. This will make the process a fruitful journey and help him to reach a good state of mind for progress.

One of the wonders in coaching is the flexibility of approaches and the tools available for helping the client evolve along his journey. Don't limit your client by limiting yourself as a coach!

36. What are the most common mistakes in goal-setting?

Setting a goal isn't difficult. However, some mistakes are stumbling blocks if you are not careful. Listed below are the most common mistakes in goal setting:

- Not knowing what you want;
- Setting a goal just because you think you should;
- Taking on too much;
- Not taking the consequences into account;
- Lack of a time frame;
- Lack of imagination;
- Setting a goal that is not really your own.

Some clients don't know what they want. Some people get anxious and nervous about life on a day-to-day basis but when they are asked about their game plan they don't have one. This is where a coach can help clients see what they want.

There are several exercises to use. One of them is the popular wheel of life shown in diagram 1.

This diagnostic tool helps the client to understand what is happening in their lives at this precise moment in time. The wheel is flexible and can be adapted to fit the clients' focus areas of life. The client is asked to divide the circle into as many components as there are areas of his life at the moment. The size of each component depends on its importance right now. Once the client has identified the core components of the wheel he assesses each one using a scale of one to ten, with ten being the highest, and indicates that the client feels completely fulfilled in that area. Remember the scale reflects the client's views in relation to each component. The coach's job is to observe and probe, not to provide his opinion. When the wheel is established the client can choose areas to focus upon in more detail.

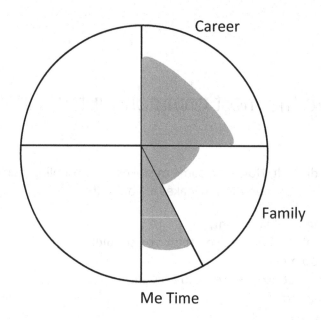

Diagram 1 – Wheel of Life

Another way to help the client realise his deepest desires is simply to ask questions:

- What do you really want in life?
- What difference does 'X' make in your life?
- What impact would achieving this goal have?
- Using a scale one to ten, with ten being the highest, how important is that to you?

There are other exercises that help clients get in touch with what they want. One kind is **visualisation**. After relaxing, the client is asked to visualise his goal. The coach asks various questions about the scene the client is imagining, such as who is present, what he can hear and how he feels. Another kind is making a **treasure map**. The client collects pictures from magazines and newspapers to show the life he wants to live and sticks them on a blank piece of paper. While visualisation may work better for a visual person, the treasure map may resonate more with a kinaesthetic individual.

Our unconscious minds can sabotage us and it's not uncommon to think we *should* have something, *should* do something or *should* be something. The use of *should* is normally a sign that part of our lives is not going well. Pay attention to what the client says when talking about his goal and challenge him to realise its importance.

Being overwhelmed with too many things to do is a very common complaint in these modern times. To prevent clients from taking on too much, here are a few tips. First, help them to break down their goal into mini-goals and small sub-tasks. Note that it's helpful to work the goal backwards. For example, map out what needs to happen in one year's time, nine-months, six-months, etc., to achieve a goal. Setting a reward for achieving each step is also a successful motivational trick that works well with many people.

Secondly, ask your client the following questions:

- If you work in one area of your life alone, which one would make the biggest difference?
- What might happen if you focus on all the goals at once?
- What time frame works best?
- What has worked for you in the past?

This last question is very important to help you discover their goal-setting history and successful achievements.

Turning a blind eye to the consequences of a goal is definitely a common mistake that often leads to big repercussions if not addressed. Asking clients a few reality questions helps them consider the knock-on effects of their goals.

- What could be the possible consequences if you were to achieve this?
- What can you do to ensure this will not happen?

Notice the future tense in the second question ('will'), instead of the present tense. It gives the client hope that things can still work out.

A goal lacking a time frame is doomed to fail. Make sure your client sets an actual date for achieving a goal. Help him organise the necessary actions for making this goal a reality. The time frame needs to be realistic. Once the client has put a date on the goal ask him "How realistic is that?" Ask him to assess the answer on a scale of one to ten.

Not engaging the imagination is another mistake that prevents individuals from reaching their goals. Goals need to be SMART, PURE and CLEAR[5], and the client must take into consideration what might be different when the goal is achieved. What can coaches do to ensure the client's imagination is fully engaged? The best exercises are visualisations that take into consideration the use of sensory terms, in order to connect with visual, auditory and kinaesthetic people. Using the present tense when doing this exercise makes the goal nearer and possible to achieve. Challenging clients to think 'outside the box', within the safe environment of a coaching session is a first step to tapping into their imagination.

Clients sometimes have a tendency to set goals that don't resonate with them. Boldly asking the question "Whose goal are you trying to achieve?" may do the trick. Soften the question with an appropriate tone of voice. Examples in life are weight loss and career choices. However, in the corporate world a client is often given a goal that is not his. Nevertheless he needs to achieve it.

---

5. SMART stands for Specific, Measured, Action oriented, Realistic, Time bound. PURE stands for Positively stated, Understood, Rel evant, Ethical CLEAR stands for Challenging, Legal, Environmentally friendly, Appropriate, Recorded.

In these cases the coach helps by assisting him to recognise the benefits of achieving the goal, to look at his values and to understand the motivation behind reaching the goal.

37. How can you help clients go from dream list to goal list?

The main differences between a dream list and a goal list are timescales and action planning. A dream list is nothing more than a wish list. If not acted upon it remains an eternal longing. On the other hand, a goal list is more structured and planned.

Helping clients go from a *dream list* to a goal list is one of the most vital supports coaches provide. The first step in the transformation is talking about the dream and converting it into something attainable. This step is called goal setting.

Goal setting can be an important step in a coaching session. Goals help the client to visualise fulfilment in his life and ultimately help him decide what he wants to achieve. In addition, setting goals lets both the client and the coach know where they are going and when they have reached the achievement. An important piece of the puzzle is congruence between the goal and the client's core values. A useful tip in coaching practices is to involve the client in a values elicitation exercise, before considering setting long-term goals (see question 49).

There are four types of goals:

- **Go up** goals;
- **Give up** goals;
- **Deficiency** goals;
- **Away from** goals.

Go up goals, also called toward goals, are linked with growth and enhancement. For example, getting a new job, a new house, a promotion or achieving an award are go up goals. Attaining something grants one step up in the staircase of life. One school of thought advises individuals to be careful when sharing go up goals because of negative external influences disguised under the 'five cancerous behaviours': criticising, complaining, comparing, competing and condemning[6]. While often unwise in a weak socio-economic environment, in some cases sharing these goals also inspires others to move forward towards defined fulfilment.

Give up goals tend to be linked with giving up something like a bad habit. To foster success, frequent encouragement is good. Hence, sharing giving up goals with others will strengthen one's circle of support and increase chances of success.

---

6. Based on *The 8th Habit* from Stephen Covey.

Deficiency goals are those that become valid once something ceases existence. One of the most common examples is health. Under threat a person acts.

Away from goals are linked with reaching an objective that takes you away from a specific situation or feeling. For example, *"I don't want to be working in this environment or with these people"*.

It is common to express an away from goal, stressing what we don't want rather than what we truly do want. Here lies one of the most recurring techniques in coaching – *rewording goals*. When an individual expresses a personal goal in the 'away from' form, the coach asks him to reword it as a 'toward goal'. By doing this the coach is allowing a positive mindset in the client so that the goal is something he is looking forward to reaching.

Reframing is a NLP technique also applied to goal setting. Stephen Covey describes it as paradigm shift in his book *7 Habits of Highly Effective People*. Reframing shifts the perspective on a given situation and enables the client to see a previously invisible opportunity.

Describing a goal as SMART, PURE and CLEAR as much as possible increases the chances of success and eases the task of exploring options for reaching the goal.

Goals are often associated with a time frame. There are long-term goals (ranging between one to three years), medium-term goals (between three months and a year) and short-term goals (between one and three months).

The co-active coaching model, developed by Whitworth, Kimsey-House and Sandahl, separates goals into those to be reached at a specific time in the future and on-going goals. In spite of this classification, the most fundamental element highlighted by the authors is the importance of breaking goals into manageable pieces. Thus, to start planning goals, one needs to begin by working backwards from long-term goals, into what needs to be achieved in a year's time, then quarterly and finally what needs to be done on a monthly or even weekly basis, in order to reach the identified milestones.

Revisiting one's goal list is a fundamental exercise. As circumstances change the hierarchy of the value system also changes. Modifications affect dreams over time and it's only human to adjust life to reach fulfilment and happiness in its new format.

Achieving goals sometimes seems like *mission impossible*. The secret lies in the correct use of the essential elements of being positive and passionate about the goal, reviewing progress on a frequent basis, getting support from friends, family members and others in or outside one's network, acquiring the skills required to reach the goal and rewarding oneself for the achievements throughout the journey. Apply these elements when you are assisting your client to move from a dream list to a goal list.

38. How can I ensure I am ready with the next question once the client has finished talking?

This is a typical question asked by new and inexperienced coaches. The coaching session is not about you, so do not put pressure on yourself regarding the next question. If you listen attentively to what the client is saying you will undoubtedly continue the interaction with a question, comment or exercise.

The trick is the mastery of four coaching skills: listening, paraphrasing, silence and intuition.

The proper level of listening in a coaching session is *focused listening* and *global listening*. If you worry about your next question, you most certainly are listening at level I - internal listening. Your self-talk is very active, breaking your concentration and diverting your attention from the client and what he is saying. For best practices on getting your attention back to the client, please read answer 42.

Your intervention doesn't necessarily have to be a question. A great deal of value is in reflecting back or paraphrasing what the client says and restating what you have heard. There is no need for interpretation. If he says something like "I hate my ex-wife", repeating that in a calm voice, without intonation, will trigger a need to elaborate the sentence. Then he can explain more of his feelings, specifically what he loathes in her, or he can say it was an exaggeration.

If you have a strong reaction to your client's words and it seems worth mentioning, do so. Let him know what you were feeling as he talked. Help draw parallels with the outside world to the feelings and reactions he gets when interacting with others.

Silence is one of the most powerful tools in coaching. Your silence is often as powerful as a question, if not more in some circumstances. Learn to give clients space to breath, to think about what they have said and to feel their reaction to their words.

Finally, learn to trust your intuition. Expressing intuition in a coaching session is very useful for showing the client your reaction to his own words and communicating with him on several levels (visual, auditory, intuitive, etc.). However, intuition is a very complex source of data that can easily get mixed up with the coach's own agenda.

The authors of *Co-Active Coaching Model* wrote about the concept of *"dancing in the moment"*. It's one of the best metaphors when it comes to coaching. Let go of controlling the next question and learn how to dance in the moment. Once mastered, your next move will come naturally and nervousness disappears. Learning to trust and to use your skills as a coach is the best way to ensure the session flows accordingly.

39. How long should I wait before asking another question?

There is the *three second rule* which says that after any intervention you should wait at least three seconds before talking. When the client finishes speaking, wait three seconds before posing another question. Give him time to further elaborate his answer or hint that he won't be adding anything else.

In some cases three seconds is not enough. In other situations the client needs more time to think about his answer, to assess his feelings or to be quiet. When the client is emotionally venting, for example crying or shouting, calmness and silence have an extremely important impact.

Sometimes the client doesn't want to answer your question and is waiting for you to intervene. Coaching is far from a game. But in certain situations, governed by your intuition, it is interesting to understand what is behind the unwillingness to respond. Delay intervening and test the client by remaining silent. He will break the discomfort and the awkwardness of the silence.

Face-to-face coaching gives you different cues to watch for compared to telephone coaching. During a meeting in person you are able to see the client's reaction and to see his emotions surface. You will recognise whether your question needs simplification, if he is working on the answer or whether his body language provides you with information. On the phone you have silence, hesitation and breathing patterns. It's more difficult to determine when to ask your next question. On the phone, refrain from intervening before applying the three seconds rule. I guarantee that if the silence becomes too overwhelming the client will be the first to break it with something like "I am not sure what to answer" or "Could you please repeat the question?"

More is lost if you break a silence than if you extend it. The loss of breaking a silence is linked with interrupting the individual's thinking process. Interrupting his introspection and reflection sometimes causes the client to forget what he was thinking about.

Dealing with silence is something you need to master as a coach. In everyday tasks, everyone is expected to give an answer within a split second of the question being posed. Giving space and time for people to think is an art that many have not mastered. Practice is a good remedy.

40. How do I keep my attention focused?

Simply pay attention. The best way to pay attention is through active listening – really listen to what the client is saying and reflect that back to them. That's it! Consider what the reasons are behind your lack of attention. Does your client's issue make you wonder about your own life? Does it trigger another state of mind? As part of an open and honest relationship with the client, mention your struggle to keep up with what he is saying. It may reveal a parallel with people in his life and create another insight.

If the situation is experienced often and with more than one client it is important to analyse it more deeply. If it occurs too often it may have more to do with you than with your clients. Getting yourself a coach or discussing the matter with your supervisor would be a wise step. Allow yourself to be challenged and face up to subconscious thinking patterns.

Keep yourself up to date with the latest meditation techniques and find ways to enhance your preparation before a coaching session. Free up your mind and learn to only focus on the client's issues.

Refer to answer 42 for further reading about how to focus your attention back to the client.

41. What is the best way to remember what the client just said?

Pay attention and listen intently to what the client says and reflect this back to them. Some coaches have a notepad with them in case they want to jot down some of the words the client uses or any other comments. That is helpful for remembering what the client said without interrupting him.

Another less conventional way is to associate some of the things the client is saying with your own imagery. For instance, when a client compares a feeling to a flower you immediately imagine a rose. It's your interpretation, but it may be easier to remember what he was talking about. This is a tricky process because you might easily fall into your own generalisations and interpretations of events.

You can also associate what has been said with the client's body language, facial expression or hand gestures. Combined with their words it may make it easier to recall what was said.

Requesting that the client repeats what was said is helpful, although less professional. It is good to ask the client to summarise and that gives you the opportunity to learn from their recap and to refocus your attention.

42. How can the coach refocus his or her attention once concentration is lost?

Some coaches use the following tricks when they lose concentration on what the client is saying:

- Take a few deep breaths and adjust yourself in your seat;
- Drink some water;
- Focus your attention on the client's posture;
- Tap your tongue to the roof of your mouth without making a noise;
- Ask the client to recap what has been discussed so far;
- Be honest.

Loss of concentration is linked with poor brain oxygenation. Taking a few deep breaths using all of your lung power will help you re-establish concentration. Checking and adjusting your posture revitalises muscles that are too relaxed.

Cool water refreshes your cells, giving you a few moments to compose yourself and to refocus on the client.

Shift your mind from your thoughts to what the client is saying by focusing on his posture and observing what isn't being said. Focus your eyes on how the client is speaking, the way he uses his hands, his facial and body expressions and the way he is sitting. Feedback to him what you have observed, using questions, such as "What's happening to you now?" or "What do you notice about how you are sitting?"

Tapping your tongue on the roof of your mouth will trigger a brain reaction and bring you back to the present. Then shift your attention to the client.

Asking the client to recap what has been discussed gives you a second chance to hear what is said and to register its meaning. Observe the way he talks when summarising. Tone and body language give you additional information for a deeper probe.

Be honest with your client and let him know your attention has drifted. Ask if there is any parallel to be drawn between the *here and now* and your own lack of concentration, and the *there and then,* when he interacts with other people. Often similarities explain some of the reactions the client receives at work from his peers or from his spouse and other family members. Once your session has finished it is important to revisit the reasons behind your *drift away* moment. How can you prevent it from happening again? It is also an important topic to address during one of your supervision talks.

43. In an executive coaching context, what should be reported back to the sponsor?

In an executive coaching process, progress and final reviews are important milestones. Sponsors often expect you to report back everything regarding your coaching sessions with the client. While it is important to keep the sponsor aware of your progress your loyalty is also to the individual client. Before reporting anything to the sponsor confer with your client, who is the person receiving coaching. Some executive coaches believe the progress meetings and final meetings should be held between the three parties involved and the update should be given by the client. If that is not possible, create a short report about how the individual is moving forward with the goals previously set and agreed upon. This report should be written and approved by the client. That is a failsafe way to ensure you don't break confidentiality by mistake. Often the sponsor will try to get more information from you. If so, beware of your own comments in the corridor and in lunch talk. Your confidentiality agreement is, above all, with the client.

Typically, the report includes:

- Progress related to the contracted set goal;
- Action planning developed by the client;
- Differences in the client's behaviour;
- Mention of the exercises applied (optional because it may be misinterpreted by an outsider);
- Any topic the client wishes to raise in the meeting.

For quantitative goals showing the most up-to-date measurements is often well perceived, as are visual aids. These can assist the sponsor with understanding the client's progress and confirm that coaching is a great managerial tool. For qualitative goals, such as behavioural changes, sharing observations and giving feedback, are the best way to proceed with the meeting.

In any triangular scenario make it clear from the start that the client may decide to leave the company as a result of the self-discovery process. If that's the case it is not your responsibility to bring this to the attention of the sponsor. It is the client's responsibility.

For the final meeting it is helpful to highlight other ways clients can get support, such as through their own support network or an ongoing coaching relationship with you via telephone or email. After the initial engagement, it is common for the coach to visit the client once (after four to six months) to assess progress.

44. What can I do to maximise learning?

Before we go into detail about where you can learn more about coaching and other practices it is worthwhile to reflect on the act of learning.

Kolb's concept was that learning is a cyclical process which contains four elements: Feeling, Watching, Thinking and Doing. Based on that, he identified four learning styles for enabling real comprehension to take place: Diverging, Assimilating, Accommodating and Converging. This was one of the major contributions to management in general. Based on his great work, Honey and Mumford created their own learning style model as shown in diagram 2.

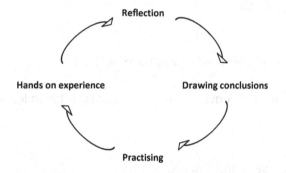

Diagram 2 –Learning cycle based on Honey and Mumford's model

In their model, Honey and Mumford renamed the learning styles to:

- **Activists** – Do - "I'll try anything at least once!"
- **Reflectors** – Review - "I'd like to think about it."
- **Theorists** – Conclude - "How does A fit in with B?"
- **Pragmatists** – Plan - "How can I apply this?"

Just as some individuals have a preference for how to learn, learning activities are strongly geared towards one of these four learning styles. When the individual's preference and the learning activity have matching styles he is more likely to learn. When it's not the case the individual is much less likely to learn.

Below are various actions that help maximise learning:

- Identify preferred learning style(s);
- Review how the styles help learning in day-to-day activities;
- Review learning skills and how to develop them further;
- Look at all learning options and test each one for learning opportunities;
- Set a time aside each day or week to identify what was learned.

Once you have identified the style and know how to maximise learning choose matching activities. Below is a list of activities likely to improve learning in each specific style. Have them in mind when choosing where and what to do to learn more about coaching and related practices.

Activist Style
- Doing presentations;
- Leading discussions;
- Attending mastermind classes;
- Competitive teamwork tasks;
- Role-play exercises;
- Involvement with other people through problem solving and sharing ideas.

Reflector Style
- Watching videos and films;
- Reading;
- Research;
- Time to prepare and review what you have learned;
- Report writing;
- Probing, usually in a safe environment, within a structured learning experience.

Theorist Style
- Exploring relating ideas and situations;
- Questioning and probing basic methodology and logic;
- Tutorial sessions;
- Reading or listening to audio information.

Pragmatist Style
- Techniques with practical application;
- Practise situations with the help of an expert;
- Demonstration from someone with a proven track record;
- Examples and anecdotes;
- Simulation of real problems;
- Immediate implementation opportunities;
- Drawing up action plans.

45. Where can I learn more about coaching and related practices?

After identifying your own learning style, I suggest you list places and activities for learning more about coaching and other related practices, such as NLP, Cognitive Behavioural Therapy, Positive Psychology, Reiki, Gestalt, Rogerian Argument, Transactional Analysis and more. The list below isn't exhaustive:

- Participate in Mastermind Classes with groups in the chosen field;
- Read and research in libraries and on the Internet;
- Attend seminars and workshops;
- Register for courses on themes you would like to learn more about;
- Subscribe to supervision classes on a specific practice;
- Watch videos and films on websites and elsewhere;
- Test yourself;
- Learn with a group of colleagues;
- Practise through writing essays and taking part in live activities;
- Learn from the example of others and from experience in the field;
- Attend tutorials;
- Listen to audio classes;
- Take part in simulations;
- Watch demonstrations;
- Discuss and debate with others;
- Summarise what you have learned;
- Attend introduction days;
- Talk to experts;
- Join professional associations.

46. How can NLP enrich coaching?

NLP is a methodology used in the field of modelling, meaning copying behaviour. It was developed by Richard Bandler and John Grinder in the early 70s in California. They studied experts in the fields of therapy, hypnotherapy and human change before they developed modelling techniques, such as the Meta Model and the Milton Model, which started NLP. Through these models they created processes for learning how certain things link to behavioural changes and the human mind. Since then their teachings have spread around the world and have become one of the most popular methodologies and techniques for accelerating human change.

John Grinder said *"NLP is the process of creating models of excellence. Modelling is the complex activity of capturing in a learnable transferable code the differences that make a difference between an excellent performer and an average performer, between an excellent work and an average one..."*

NLP has numerous successful uses in the following areas:

- Business – Sales, negotiation, team work, presentations, building relationships, conflict resolution, managing people;
- Education – learning and teaching, improving spelling;
- Health – weight loss, allergies, anxiety, stop smoking;
- Therapy – phobias and resolving inner conflicts;
- Coaching;
- Sport.

NLP provides additional support for enriching your coaching practice. For example, you can learn more about how the human brain functions and about the basics of epistemology - the science of how human beings communicate. NLP also helps your coaching with techniques of observation and rapport building. Bandler and Grinder realised that people make minute facial changes from moment to moment and that split second facial movements have meaning. If you have enough sensory acuity to notice them you can interpret what the person is feeling. They have developed the BLESS technique, which includes observation of the following aspects:

- **B**reathing – rate of breathing and location, high/low part of the lungs;
- **L**ower Lip Size – existence of lines;
- **E**yes – focus and pupil dilation;
- **S**kin Tonus – muscles tensed or relaxed;
- **S**kin Colour Change – blushing.

Other important observation points are tilt of the head, eyebrow movement, lip and mouth movements, the angle of the spine and hand gestures clusters.

For every single facial expression there is a meaning. Feeding back what you see, and maybe your interpretation, to the client enhances your coaching session and may help the client to open up to you. Below is a simple chart for interpretating some expressions that may be of interest when you are coaching:

Facial Expression	Interpretation
Holding breath	Anxiety
Eye pupil dilated	Arousal, Fear
Chin up, smile, chest up	Pride
Repetition of words and higher pitch	Lie
Quick intake of air	Panic
Look sideways	Recalling a memory
Fisting	Anger, Fury
Deep swallow	Strong emotion
Press lips together	Sign of hiding something
Nose wrinkle	Disgust

For further reading on NLP, read *Words that Change Minds* by Shelle Rose Charvet and *Timeline Therapy and the Basis of Personality* by Tad James. Both explore Meta programmes and other NLP fundamentals.

47. What are clean language questions and when should they be asked?

Clean Language was created by David Grove, a New Zealand therapist, in the 90's. The main objective of *Clean Language* is helping clients explore their internal metaphors and to understand their ways of thinking, as well as motivating and assisting them to change. The basic idea is to minimise the coach's own words and to use the client's words to guide exploration of fears and phobias. It also helps improving communication and rapport and provides valuable information about the way the client thinks and how they interact. Finally, it helps people make changes in their lives.

Clean questions are fundamentally subdivided into three groups, the most common being the first ones:

- **Developing questions**
  o And what kind of X (is that X)?
  o And is there anything else about X?

- **Sequence and source questions**
  o And then what happens? Or And what happens next?
  o And what happens just before X?

- **Intention questions**
  o And what would X like to have happened?
  o And what needs to happen for X?

where X is substituted with the client's words.

These are very powerful questions and I strongly advise you to read *Clean Language* by Wendy Sullivan and Judy Rees.

In ordinary coaching, the best time to pose clean questions can be when the client introduces a metaphor about his feelings. Using clean questions such as "What kind of X is that X?" and "That's X like what?"can be helpful.

Clean language is useful when the client talks about something in metaphorical terms and uses expressions such as "It's like he's an elephant walking on lilies" or "I feel like I am on a roller coaster". In these examples, you could pose clean questions like "And is there anything else about roller coaster?" or "And where is the elephant?"or "And whereabouts are the lilies?" There are endless situations where the client uses metaphors and after hearing one you can ask clean questions to keep him exploring his metaphorical world, hence learning more about themselves. To learn more about how clean language is an effective tool in exploring metaphors, please refer to answer 73.

It is wise to ask the client's permission before conducting an authentic clean language session. However, it is relevant to mention that in order to conduct an authentic clean language session you need training. It may be a little over the top for some people because of the simplicity and repetitive questioning. However, if you just intend to pose a few of these questions during your coaching session permission isn't required.

Clean language is very powerful. The simple techniques can be used in other means of communication for easy and rapid interaction with others, such as in online messenger and chat rooms.

Clean language is not only used in coaching, but in other situations such as therapy, healthcare, recruitment, sales, education, training and parenting and it can yield very fruitful results.

48. Which is better, face-to-face coaching or telephone coaching?

Gerard O'Donovan, president of the IIC, says 90% of coaching is done over the phone or through the internet. Whilst this is more likely to represent the USA market with regards to life coaching, studies show that in the UK it is more likely to be around 40%. Notwithstanding that, it is a personal choice. But, before selecting the style for your practice, compare the advantages and disadvantages. The advantages of telephone coaching are:

- Reduces accommodation and travelling expenses;
- Facilitates contact between clients and coaches located in different places;
- Client and coach relax in the comfort of their homes or offices;
- Faster reply support system through email.

However, telephone coaching demands more from the coach since he has limited opportunities to observe the client's body language and facial expressions. In this context the body language is restricted to voice, intonation, volume, pitch and pace, use of silence, hesitations and breathing patterns.

Active listening skills can be applied to perfection, coupled with the practitioner's intuition. The combination provides the coach with the knowledge to direct the conversation and explore the client's issue.

The advantages of face-to-face coaching are:

- Access to the client's full body language and facial expressions;
- Certain techniques and exercises are easier to apply;
- Able to pick up on nuances from client feedback;
- More options for rapport building;
- Ambient noise levels are better controlled.

Both types of coaching are subject to distractions and self-talk. Proper preparation and self-management at your end are essential for a successful coaching session. You will have to advise the client to select a quiet environment away from noise and distractions for successful long-distance sessions. The advantages of telephone coaching are not necessarily the disadvantages of face-to-face coaching, and visa-versa.

49. What are my coaching values?

Values are personal rules, determining who we are, how we feel and how we think. They build our identity and live in our unconscious, subconscious and conscious mind. The principles are exclusive - our essence and juice of life. They make us question things when in danger and they act like as an internal alarm system. Once something or someone steps on them they send a signal to the mind and heart. The signal is disguised as feelings, such as sadness, frustration and impatience. Physical pain and a rise in tension and stress levels are common. Lack of energy and even body dysfunctions may occur when values are not honoured. Signals are also concealed as negative thoughts, reducing motivation and, ultimately, our happiness. Once this alarm is triggered it's time to take stock and analyse what is not going well and what is blocking personal values.

Similarly coaches have coaching values. The values define the coaching, making it different from competitors. It builds a link to you.

To know your coaching values do a values elicitation exercise. It's a simple but thorough process. Once you understand what's important to your coaching, you will make connections between certain events and better understand the questions you ask clients during your sessions. The aim is to provide you with clarity concerning your coaching. You may be tempted to reply with *chunk words*[7]. You need to use more meaningful words and appropriate questioning skills on yourself. For instance, money is not a value in itself. You can replace 'money' with 'financial security' and/ or 'freedom'. Family could be simplified by using 'love', 'protection' and 'safety'.

Some values may seem more important than others to you and possibly they are. Values elicitation exercises also provide a hierarchy of values, which in turn determines the driving forces between values and raises awareness of what really matters to you.

A value elicitation exercise has three stages. Stage one asks the following question:

What is important to you when you are coaching?

Keep asking this question, until you have a list of approximately six to eight words.

Stage Two entails the comparison between values. Ask yourself:

Which value is more important to me, A or B?

---

7. Chunk Words are words that can have different meanings. They can be simplified by breaking into words that represent only one thing.

Remain neutral and stick to the question. Replacing the above question with *"Is A more important than B for me?"* will slightly emphasise A over B.

Once all values are compared, you enter Stage Three and list the values in descending order. The final product is a list headed by the most important values for you to use when coaching, for example honesty, integrity, recognition and trust.

Coaches are advised to perform values elicitation exercises for their coaching and personal value systems, to recognise the connection with their goals. If they stumble upon limiting beliefs, getting a coach is the first step to moving forward.

50. How important is it to be clear about my own 'forbidden territories'?

'Forbidden territories' are topics you would rather not discuss or debate with others. So they become blind spots and you unconsciously ignore them. This can lead to avoiding the topic with your client when it could be a breakthrough in his own journey. Your non-judgmental approach to coaching may become blurred and you may lose your impartiality towards a subject. That may ultimately impact your ability to coach.

These subjects can range from love relationships, divorce and abortion to drugs and alcohol, or to something else you are uncomfortable discussing and wish to keep in the past. Or the topic may take you out of your depth. In that case referring the client to specialised help is the best option.

Why is it so important to be clear about your own 'forbidden territories'? Because they can affect:

1. The quality of your coaching;

2. Your reputation in the marketplace;

3. Your own journey as a human being.

If you are unsure of your 'forbidden territories' then you are also uncertain about your own comfort zone. Consequently, self-management will be poorly handled and you won't know where to stop coaching and refer your client to someone else. This hinders the quality of your coaching and may cause serious repercussions.

One repercussion is for the reputation your coaching practice has in the marketplace. Once your image is dented through bad word-of-mouth marketing (one of the most powerful marketing tools) it is very hard to get back in the game.

Despite the fact that you must remain open about your issues within your profession it is advisable for you to get your own coach (or even therapy, if required) to deal with your own demons and take action to tackle them. As soon as these are tackled your comfort zone is likely to expand. That in turn will aid your coaching relationships.

However, this inner transformation takes time. It is not a matter of a few hours with your therapist or coach. For any successful change to happen, it must come from within.

51. Who can help me practise coaching?

Coaching is a discipline that requires practice in order to improve and enhance one's skills. There are people who can help you practise your coaching. Typically, when a coach is still in training practise coaching comes from pro-bono clients, in other words clients who agree to complimentary coaching sessions.

Family members and friends may be more than happy to lend time in exchange for free coaching sessions. Decide if you are comfortable coaching your family and friends.

Coaching networks can also help with your practice. Some will be willing to work with you on a co-coaching approach: you coach them and they coach you. Sessions can be organised at convenient times. The level of knowledge from coaches who belong to these networks varies considerably. Therefore you can also benefit from someone more experienced in the field.

Consider attending coaching events where you can easily meet others who want to participate in pro-bono or paid coaching. Obviously, people respond well to free coaching, but be clear about the pro-bono arrangement. Once the client has experienced the life-changing help you offer they may be more than willing to pay for continued coaching sessions.

Coaching forums and organisations normally have a list of participants. Go through those lists and identify the individuals with whom you would like to create a bond. I am sure that some will be receptive to helping you practise your skills with them.

Other untapped sources of coachees are charities and fundraising organisations. Working on a pro-bono basis with a charity is a win-win situation for you since, besides practising your skills, you are helping the organisation get better results and contributing to its members living happier lives.

A more far-fetched idea is to get in contact with gyms and sport centres to explore the possibility of helping their members with their personal fitness goals, as well as other issues they may have. Speak to the managers or approach members directly. Some would be glad to have extra support for achieving their objectives.

Remember, an innovative mindset and comfort with approaching people directly and selling yourself is key. Once you are on top of your game these pro-bono clients can easily become paying clients.

52. At the beginning of a session, what should I mention about contracting?

Before starting a coaching session there are a few points that must be mentioned to the client for the sake of contracting and code of ethics. It is important to differentiate the preparation phase from the contracting phase. The former entails techniques for enhancing your self-management and for preparing yourself as a coach for the coaching session. The contracting phase corresponds to the first few minutes of the coaching session when the coach highlights points relevant during and after the session.

The contracting points are:

- The time the session begins;
- The duration of the session;
- The confidentiality agreement;
- Client agreement on which topics will be discussed as material for your supervision or for your further developmental training;
- Note keeping method the client wishes to use;
- Asking permission about recording the session (especially for telephone calls);
- Consent for a third party to remain in the room or on the call, as part of your supervision process.

Mentioning the time and the duration at the start of the session gives a structured approach to the client and pre-warns him or her about the time they have for focusing on their issues and challenges. If you worry that this will be awkward, don't do it. After a few tries, it comes naturally.

Confidentiality is a fundamental pillar of your relationship with clients. It is imperative that you bring it up as a constant reminder, not only for the client, but also for yourself.

Get an agreement about making references to the session at a later stage as part of your developmental training or discussion points on supervision classes. The reasons for doing so are twofold:

1. It shows that you are in constant development as a coach and also have supervision;
2. It honours the bond of trust and respect between you and the coachee.

Constant development, training and supervision are nothing to be ashamed of. In fact, the opposite is true. If you are concerned about what people may think of you, such as that you are still in the qualification process, you should pre-empt any preconceived ideas that you suspect your clients may have by clearly stating otherwise. Clients like to work with people who are transparent and constantly deepening their knowledge. Anyway, you probably only have to explain this once and then just get his or her agreement in every session.

Note-keeping is important for later when reflecting upon what has been said. Some clients are so nervous about what they want to share that they forget the relevance of having pen and paper in front of them. A simple reminder posed as a question will discretely bring it to light. In addition, a coach often likes to take notes as well. Simply mention it at the beginning of the session using, "I hope you don't mind me taking some notes during the session" or "Is it ok with you if I make some notes during the session?"

Similarly, when you are planning to record telephone coaching, you need the client's agreement beforehand, for the sake of transparency and honesty within your coaching relationship. Nowadays with the development of technology it is very easy to record the session without the client's knowledge. Asking permission reassures him that you are serious about your own development as a coach, that you value his opinion and don't want to breach any confidentiality agreement and that you respect your code of ethics. It helps to explain to the client the reasons why you would want to record the telephone call. These are typically for: self-development, supervision or accreditation purposes. It is useful to mention that you can also share the tape or file with him for his own records. If the answer is a no, you will have to respect the client's wishes and not record the session. If you carry on anyway with the recording and the client finds out, it burns a lot of bridges within the relationship and you will be lucky if the client doesn't terminate the coaching engagement!

Finally, when your supervisor attends your coaching sessions, coaching etiquette recommends that you talk to your clients beforehand and get their agreement before proceeding. On the day of the evaluation, just remind your clients of your previous agreement and introduce your supervisor at the beginning of the call or the meeting.

In summary, the contracting part of a session is very important, since it provides a framework for the session and emphasises the pillars of a trustworthy relationship – transparency and honesty.

53. What is the best policy regarding taking notes during a coaching session?

This is one of those subjects where the coach's own judgement is key. On one hand, there are numerous experienced coaches who argue that record keeping must be reduced to a minimum, for example to the session's goal and homework. On the other hand, there are others who believe keeping records of the complete list of discussed options and any recurring expression (on top of notes regarding goal and requests) is an invaluable addition to the coaching relationship.

Another school of thought believes that taking notes disturbs the pace of the session.

For Patrick Williams and Sharon Anderson, authors of *Law and Ethics in Coaching: How to Solve and Avoid Problems in Your Practice*, best practice encompasses keeping good records and documenting the coaching relationship as a safeguard in a possible dispute with the client. However, recognised voices in the coaching world disagree with this. Through their years of experience they have learned that the practitioner notes can easily be distorted and manipulated in cross-examination. Therefore, they strongly advise keeping factual notes available to the client under the Data Protection Act. Another option is to keep coded 'aide-memoirs', avoiding revealing the client's identity. These 'aide-memoirs' are not considered client notes and therefore not admissible to a court.

The truth is that when it comes to records the coach needs to act prudently. Beware of any confidentiality breach and comply with the Data Protection Act 1998[8]. It is important to keep notes that can identify your clients out of reach. Password-protect your computer files and ensure that if you keep any written or printed notes they are safely stored where only you have access.

Record keeping is relevant when practising executive and corporate coaching. Here, the organisation subcontracting the coaching services requests to be kept in the loop with action-planning and decision making, etc. Everyone involved in the executive coaching process must be made aware of this.

When practising telephone coaching, ask permission from your client to record the session. It is important to be as transparent as possible and to mention the reasons behind wanting to record the phone calls.

---

8. This is a set of regulations on the proper management of processing personal information. Any coaching practice must notify their national Information Commissioner's Office of the data handled and failure to do so can be considered an offence.

The most recurrent reason is training purposes, so at a later stage you can listen to the conversation once again and analyse other ways and methods you could have used in that session. Additionally, clients are sometimes interested in listening to their own telephone coaching sessions, which helps them in their reflection process.

54. What should I do when the session is running over time?

It is your responsibility as a coach to time-manage the session accordingly. It is acceptable to prolong the session for another five to ten minutes maximum. Presumably neither you nor the client wants the session to extend indefinitely.

Pay attention to the time spent during a coaching session and know when it is likely to run late before the last minute. If you realise you are running late, use one of the following interventions:

- "Being conscious of time, I would like to accelerate the process to...";
- "In order not to delay the end of our session, my last question is...";
- "We are getting closer to the end of the session: how would you like to use our last minutes?"
- "Time is coming up very soon: what actions will you take on today?."

This will change the speed of the session and give the client the choice to act quickly.

When scheduling meetings with your clients, give yourself enough time to prepare in between sessions and to accommodate any delays. Many coaches book coaching sessions with extra half-hour intervals in between, which provides plenty of time to prepare, ventilate the room, take a break and manage any delays.

If your time management skills are a bit rusty, improve them. Tips include:

- Sit where you can discreetly check the time;
- Take action once you get pulled off track.

In a coaching session it's quite common for the client to wander off track. While the new subject may be related to the current session (and help its progress in some way) it may well be the opposite. Simply asking the client *"What impact does this have on reaching the session's goal?"* or *"In what way does this relate to the goal?"* may bring the client back. Another way of moving the session forward is through the use of interventions just before a question, such as *"Reflecting back at your goal for this session, how / what / when...?"*

When the new information is important to the long-term goal, but is distracting the current session's goal, the coach can reinforce the goal for that session and explicitly say the new topic can be the subject of a different session. However, in order to build confidence in the coaching relationship, coach John Whitmore advises the coach to follow the coachee's storyline rather than his own train of thought. This will make the client feel his interest and needs are being respected. Once again, for me, the answer lies in the moment and the coach must decide what is best for that specific case.

55. What are the different kinds of questions I could use in coaching sessions?

A question is an invitation to share information or an opinion with others. The skill lies in choosing the appropriate invitation to elicit the type of response you seek. There are two types of questions:

- **Open** – Offering the respondent a wide choice of answers. Open questions start with What, Why, When, Who, Where or How;

- **Closed** – Offering the respondent a limited number of choices (normally yes or no). These questions tend to start with Is, Can, Have, Will, Do. Some variations of How, such as 'how many?' or 'how often?' can also be considered as closed questions.

Within the open questions field, several categories exist:

- **Questions for directing attention** – These are straightforward, but very powerful, e.g. "When a colleague is aggressive, what is it that you notice about them?"

- **Questions for clarification** – These questions are designed to:

   a) Clarify the coach's understanding, usually on terminology. For example, "Sorry, what exactly do you mean by mashie nugget?"

   b) Make things clearer to the client. For example, "From what you just said, your family comes second with regards to your work. What makes it that way?"

- **Questions that tie things down** – Normally used to get commitment from the client. For example, "From this list, which one thing will you commit to doing and by when?"

- **Questions that challenge current thinking** – This type of question tends to change current thinking patterns, e.g. "What happens if things don't work out the way you think they will?"

- **Questions that change minds** – Challenging questions invite the client to think 'outside the box', e.g. "What else could you interpret from your boss's behaviour?"

- **Incisive questions** – This is an alternative way to handle limiting beliefs. It invites the client to think *as if* they didn't have the limiting beliefs. For example, "If you didn't care with others' opinions, what would you do?"

According to the International Coaching Federation (ICF), powerful questions are divided into five main groups:

- **Situational questions** - These questions have the objective of obtaining information. Typically, they start with questions like How, When and Where;

- **Motivational questions** – Their objective is to discover what moves the client. Examples are: "What is important for you?" or "Where does your preference lie?"

- **Implying questions** – With the objective of connecting cause and effect, such as "What would happen if...?" or "What is the impact of X?"

- **Possibility questions** – These questions take the client to generate several options to solve his problem, as for example in, "What would the best possible result be?" or "Imagine that Y is possible. Knowing what you know now, what would you do to attain a better result?"

- **Sensorial questions** – These explore feelings, very much on these lines, "How did you feel when you said that?"

When asking any of the types of questions above, there are some nuances to take in consideration:

- **Leading questions** – These questions put words in the speaker's mouth and should therefore be avoided. For example, "No one would pay attention to you in those circumstances, would they?" Don't impose your own interpretation;

- **Use of voice tonality** – Your voice tone when asking a question impacts the person who is listening to you. Notice the level of empathy, authority and challenge used when you pose a question to others. The intention is to trigger reflection, not fear;
- **Use Silence** – People react differently to questions: they need time to think about the answer. Exercise patience when asking a question and give the client time to think about how and what he wants to answer. Silence does not necessarily mean he doesn't have an answer, or that he didn't understand the question. Search for clues in his body language;

- **Simple questions** – When questioning, try to simplify your questions as much as possible and avoid asking more than one question at the same time;

- **Use of presuppositions or 'slide-past'** – Include presuppositions within the question to help your client move their thinking forward and to by-pass any obstacles. For example, "What resources do you need to acquire so that you can achieve this goal?" This question implies the client can acquire extra resources and that he or she can reach the goal.

In summary, probing is a skill that requires special consideration but that when done properly can transform lives and spark positive change. This skill can be improved with practice.

56. When is it useful to ask closed questions during a coaching session?

There are a few times during a coaching session when a closed question may be appropriate. These are normally related to administrative aspects of the session and are linked to bold questioning techniques.

During both the beginning and end of the coaching session there are contractual points relevant to emphasise. The list below highlights some of the situations where a closed question is well suited:

Beginning of the session

- Taking notes during meeting;
- Recording telephone sessions;
- Asking if the client would like any refreshment;
- Checking levels of light, temperature and noise in the room;
- Getting agreement to reference to the session as training material at a later stage.

End of the session

- Scheduling next appointment;
- Requesting homework to be done;
- Asking if the client would like your notes or the records of the call;
- Closing the session.

In all of these moments a closed question will be adequate. These start with a verb, like for example:

- "Would you like a glass of water?"
- "Is the room's temperature ok for you?"
- "Do you mind if I write some notes on my notepad during the session?"
- "Will you do this exercise before the next session?"

Of course all of these can also be transformed into open questions. However, sometimes it feels unnatural and gives too many choices for the client, when a simple yes or a no is enough.

Another context when closed questions are acceptable is when you challenge the client. Obviously, there are several different types of methods for challenging clients and some involve plenty of open questions. However, when a client is affirming something contradicted by his body language, the coach can calmly pose a closed question, such as: "Is it so?", "Are you sure?", "Do you believe in that?" or simply "Really?" These simple interventions will hint your disbelief about his words and will also allow him to elaborate and, in some cases, open up totally. In some situations a short explanation of the mismatch and incongruence you observe, between their words and their body language, is helpful.

When challenging clients, ask closed questions in an adequate voice tone - nothing too harsh, aggressive or patronising, but somehow calm. Sometimes even humour can make him feel safe enough to confide his fears and limiting beliefs.

57. What type of questions should I avoid in a coaching session?

There is a school of thought within the coaching industry which argues that the number of closed questions used should be limited, as they don't enable clients to elaborate their answers and develop their progress. Moreover, sometimes closed questions carry a hidden message, as if implying the questioner's own opinion. That is why closed questions should be limited to administrative aspects of the session or bold questioning techniques (read answer 52 for more about administrative points within a coaching session).

Other types of questions to avoid are those that start with *'why'*. Even though this is considered an open question, it triggers defensiveness and justification from the client and creates an unnecessary level of tension in the coaching session. Try replacing *'why'* for *'what reason(s) did you do X?'*

The most effective questions start with What, Where, When, Who and How much/many. They seek to quantify and gather facts, while 'why', and in some cases 'how' questions invite analysis and opinion, implying defensiveness, criticism, judgement and pressure, which eventually hinders the coaching relationship.

Sometimes 'why' questions can be posed within a coaching environment in order to get an effective outcome but beware of your tone of voice. Experienced coaches suggest using a calm voice tone with a hint of caring and support.

In her book Linda Metcalf mentions an interesting and simple question she refers to as the 'miracle question'. It is a question that guides the client to think about what type of miracle they would like to experience in their lives, at that precise moment in time and how that miracle would happen.

"Suppose tonight when you go to sleep a miracle happens. Tomorrow morning when you wake up, what has changed in your actions, attitudes and your way of thinking that would indicate to you that a miracle had happened?"

This is a powerful question because it invites the client to imagine what he would like to happen and what impact this would have in his daily life. This visualisation brings an invisible strength to the individual and deepens his wish to see a transformation in his life. The question shows implicitly that whatever the client desires is associated with a change in his own actions, behaviour and thinking patterns.

This question corroborates with the popular saying, *"He who does what he has always done, gets what he has always got."*

As you know, the type of vocabulary exchanged between coach and client is a fundamental element in building rapport. The miracle question may not go down so well for non-religious people and will end up wasting a great opportunity for creating a magic moment for them. Hence, the executive coach Carole Pemberton suggests altering slightly the miracle question to the following:

- What would be different for you once the problem is solved?
- What would tell you that X doesn't constitute an issue any more?
- If we get together in a month, what would you be doing differently that will indicate to me the problem has been solved?
- What would show your colleagues that X is not a problem to the team anymore?
- What would be the first sign that would indicate to other people the challenge has gone?

There isn't a right question for a given situation. Your coaching style will dictate how you pose the question.

However, best practices show that once the session has come to an end, the coach benefits from evaluating the posed questions and the way they were asked and brainstorming other ways to ask similar questions, as well as thinking about what questions that would lead to a better / different outcome.

I also recommend you read Judy Barber's book *Good Question! The Art of Asking Questions to Bring About Positive Change*. It is a book for inspiration and reference that collects together the coaching questions used by 28 experienced coaches. It shows in detail how coaches can use questions and related exercises and stories in very helpful ways.

58. What type of homework is it advisable to request in a session?

The co-active coaching model suggests the majority of actions take place between coaching sessions and that without them the balance of coaching is incomplete. Action will step into the client's life and will maintain his motivation, moving him towards his goals. Therefore giving homework to do between sessions sustains the relevance of the topics discussed and highlights that coaching is not a one-off incident without repercussions for one's life.

Be conscious of the client's life style before requesting any type of homework. Someone who is always rushing throughout the day may not have the appropriate state of mind for doing some of the exercises necessary for granting him the results he requires. On the other hand, just because someone is unemployed does not mean you can heap homework on him!

Homework must be punchy, helpful and one more milestone in the individual's journey, to be looked back upon with time and spirit.

Some exercises, such as the wheel of life or a pre-coaching form, qualify as homework, since they require time and effort to do and would be expensive for the client if done during the coaching sessions. Other exercises such as developing a powerful affirmation or searching for pictures and images for a treasure map related to personal goals are also good homework suggestions, since clients will be able to perform them in the quietness of their personal time. A common assignment many coaches request is for the client to think of a way to celebrate success. This is a task many will indulge in quite easily and proves to be an excellent way to increase self-esteem.

Assigning homework to a specific deadline, as a way towards structure and organisation, can be tricky since it depends on your client's available time. Many coaches don't give clients a deadline and simply say, "Please send me a copy when you finish." This sends the message that the coach trusts the client to finish the task in a good amount of time, without putting any pressure on them.

Some clients, on the other hand, prefer to be instructed and respond well when a deadline is established. Since you are part of that particular coaching relationship, you are in a good position to evaluate what works best with each individual client.

When you request homework from your client, keep notes of it. Then you can follow up at the beginning of the next session.

There are some clients who repeatedly don't do their homework. This will reveal a pattern. With that you have information for confronting the client about potential parallels in other areas of his life. Beware of jumping to conclusions too soon or making any assumptions.

59. How do I close a coaching session?

As with starting coaching sessions, there are ways to end coaching meetings. These are:

- Summarising the session, commenting on how initial objectives/goals set at the beginning of the session were or were not met;
- Revising the action plan;
- Checking your clients' intention, commitment and enthusiasm about actions to be performed;
- Asking the client what was gained from the session;
- Scheduling the next appointment;
- Asking if the client would like copies of your notes or call records;
- Requesting specific feedback;
- Thanking the client for their time and commitment.

Coaching is a powerful tool. It gives clients the necessary energy for changing their behaviour and attitudes based on individual choices and options and actions they defined when talking about their issues, as well as how to solve them. This is why, in order to help the client clarify all that has been said and not said, it is helpful to request the client summarise the session. A good recap is useful even if done by the coach. Nevertheless, when the client goes back over the session and he highlights what was important for him that in itself is an insight for the coach.

Similarly revising the action plan you discussed will be useful for the client. As he runs through the actions, confirming dates and ways of doing each, he identifies who could support him further to ensure implementation.

Although the coaching session is nearing its end, it does not mean the coach can relax his coaching skills. On the contrary, his skills must be as active and precise as possible. Listening skills and the use of intuition will play a crucial role in checking your client's commitment and in reading between the lines.

The 'ICE check' provides confirmation of Intention, Commitment and Enthusiasm. It is practical to quantify the client's responses by using a scale of one to ten, ten being the highest. Coaching literature reveals that any answer below a seven or eight reveals that the client is not committed. In these cases, the coach could probe which *one* action he feels would take him the next level up.

Clearly, asking the coachee about what he has gained from the session is different from summarising it. It is slightly more abstract, but it will make the client reflect on the benefits of coaching. That wraps things up nicely before asking the client when might be the best time for the next session.

Your records and notes can be given to the client. Ask him if he sees value in them before you close the session.

If you seek feedback on something specific, the end of the session is the time to request it. It's always helpful if you request feedback on specific subjects, such as questions used, exercises done, etc., instead of a broad "What did you think about the session?" question.

Finally, thanking the client for his time and commitment is coaching etiquette and subtly reinforces the bond between you two.

60. What can I do if my client becomes highly emotional during a session?

When a client shows a strong level of emotion, the wisest thing to do is to give him some time and space to deal with it. Often, clients come across strong emotions when talking about their issues and may express them by crying or raising their voice. You must remain calm and not get caught up in their behaviour. It's easy, especially when a client is crying, to jump in to save them from experiencing difficult or painful emotions. But that is not the wisest course of action - they need to deal with these difficult feelings, in their own way.

Giving time and space for the client to manage their emotions is essential. Your help, by empathically listening and reflecting on the reasons for the outburst, is welcome. Sometimes simple words, such as "Take your time" are as useful as your silence. It can do wonders to stay present and let them deal with their issues at their own pace. Because this is coaching and not therapy it is highly unlikely that the client will reach an uncontrollable state, however if you do begin to feel out of your depth then firmly but gently inform your client that this is not the style of coaching that you conduct. Alternatively, you can manage the client's level of emotional expression by shifting them into their heads and asking them to talk about or explain in more detail the reasons for the emotional situation. This engages the rational brain and is one way of containing the situation without having to stop the session.

After the client has calmed down, a bit of fresh air may help him to regain his composure. This can be done by opening a window or by going out for a short walk to a nearby park or garden.

Under no circumstances proceed with any 'touching', this may seem too cold now, as you read these lines, but it may be misinterpreted by the client and drag you into undesired consequences.

It does the client no service to quieten them. It is not professional practice to do in a coaching relationship. Let the client externalise their emotions as this may be the only safe place where they can do so.

I suggest you pay attention to your own level of anxiety and use the suggestion above to manage the situation, and then go to an experienced supervisor to help you clarify how to proceed. You may also need to go to a coach or therapist if the client's emotional outburst triggers something deep in you.

You need to remain as a sounding board for your client as this is one of the reasons he requested your services in the first place.

61. What can I do when my client keeps answering "I don't know" to my questions?

Coaching is based on the principle that the individual has the answers to his own issues and challenges. When he continually answers that he doesn't have an answer to your questions, a pattern is found.

It can be quite frustrating to be coaching someone who keeps repeating "I don't know". However, the truth is that it is unlikely to be so. One's resourcefulness, as described by the model *Coaching for Solutions* is a strong pillar and, when in an emergency situation, the client will always have a response and act upon it in some way.

The question "If you knew the answer, what would that be?" is a simple one. It may sound childish, but it is effective. It either triggers a subconscious reply or it highlights the coachee's pattern, allowing him to break it and enabling him to see he doesn't have any other choice but to answer the question. The fact is that, once asked, this question will never go unanswered.

Another interesting and effective technique is to help the client distance himself from his issue and evaluate the situation as if he were a third party or as if it has happened to a best friend who is soliciting his opinion. This technique allows the client to break free of self-imposed pressure and think 'outside the box'. His answer will be congruent with his values and he will genuinely suggest what, in his opinion, is the best for his friend. Once this is revealed some clients benefit from drawing the parallel between their friend's issue and their own. This can be achieved simply with a question, such as "What can you take from that answer to your friend about your situation?"

Another helpful method is to imagine bringing the best friend in to the session and to encourage the client to answer any question posed by the friend. This Gestalt method can be very different from how you are used to coaching, especially if your coaching model is based on process models, such as GROW. It can be very effective, mainly with clients who like 'outside the box' thinking and unusual approaches or who have an artistic bent.

Finally, another way to turn off the client's repetition is simply to repeat it out loud. You can say it in a calm way with an inquisitive intonation to it or you can just whisper. The use of adequate voice tone from your side is important to trigger their urge to elaborate on the answer.

Ultimately, you can challenge the pattern with "I have noticed you tend to answer my questions with "I don't know"". This is not a question, only an observation, which will certainly urge the client to comment. However, you can also add the following question "What are the reasons behind that?" or something to that effect, which is a more open approach.

In any of the methods explained above, you as the coach should remain calm and not let frustration take control of the situation. The session is centred on the client and his feelings, not yours.

62. What can I do if I don't feel comfortable tackling a specific subject with a client?

The coaching relationship is supposed to be based on trust and honesty between the parties.

Before answering in detail it is relevant to explore two important aspects - self management and boundaries. The first is linked with content, while the latter is associated with the context of a coaching session.

Self-management is based on the acknowledgement that some areas lie outside the coach's comfort zone, but may well form part of what is pertinent to the client and subsequent probing and challenging towards its self-discovery is paramount. The co-active coaching model goes one step further, considering the reasons why the coach would hold back from exploring these self-imposed 'forbidden territories'. These reasons could be fear of upsetting or losing the client, fear of offending the client, fear of uncovering a specific part of himself as a coach about which they feel insecure and uncomfortable, and fear of the consequences.

It is critical that the coach reflects upon these areas and reduces any emotional charge associated with them so that they can coach and guide the client to an appropriate level of action. This would be an answer to the client's issues, not those of the coach. Again we see adequate levels of preparation playing a significant part.

With regards to boundaries, coaches always operate within the limits of their own technical competence, recognise where competence has the potential to be exceeded and when it is best to refer the client to a more experienced coach or to provide them with support in seeking the help of another professional, such as a therapist, counsellor, psychiatrist, and/or business/ financial advisor.

Examples of subjects related to self-management are divorce and abortion. For boundaries the most common examples are: financial advice, sexual abuse, trauma and depression.

When the coach fails to eliminate his emotional charge and/or feels out of his depth discussing a subject or simply uncomfortable tackling it, then he needs to be honest and to inform the client of this discomfort. It's likely that the client will be surprised, but you will have honoured your relationship and your code of ethics. A referral to another coach or therapist may be necessary.

Supervision and coaching will help you understand the reasons behind these feelings of uneasiness and assist you with an adequate plan of action to deal with them in the future.

63. How can my internal dialogue be silenced?

Internal dialogue is the same as self-talk and when it is active it means you are listening at level I – internal listening.

Internal Listening is our day-to-day listening status. It focuses on oneself and allows lively self-talk. Once self-talk is active barriers for proper listening are silently constructed and the coach's attention is redirected to other matters beyond the client's agenda. When self-talk is active the coach easily diverts to rehearsing his next question, which tends to be a closed question. Very often he refers back to one of his own previous experiences related to the topic under discussion. Or the coach may jump into problem solving and advising. In addition, placating, derailing, joking, interrupting and making assumptions may suddenly and unconsciously take over. Other common problems are impatience and switching off or failing to listen at all, as soon as the coach feels satisfied with the answers received.

Internal listening is certainly not the appropriate listening level for conducting a coaching session. To control your own thoughts it is advisable to practise *clearing inner space* before a session.

This exercise is about freeing your mind from your own thoughts and judgements and being in command of your self-talk. By clearing your inner space you as a coach are in a position to receive information, the thoughts the client needs or wants to unload. After talking through the information you will then exercise questioning skills and generate opportunities for the client to recognise things in different ways and to approach the subject from different angles.

Coaching literature suggests that clearing inner space can be done through meditation, keeping a journal and/or selection of input. The last is affected by our surroundings, friends, books we read, TV/radio, etc. In turn, these influence our thoughts and beliefs. To control the input, one needs to manage the contents of our surroundings and ensure more positive input. As coach Gerard O'Donovan says *"Being aware of and getting rid of the inputs that are not adding anything to your life will help you to create space"*. This space will allow you to focus on your client and to be absorbed in his agenda.

I, personally, find meditation prior to a coaching session to be a great tool. I switch off any source of distraction and noise, close my eyes, concentrate on my breathing and focus on the coloured light I see with my eyes shut. For religious coaches, sending a little prayer to your guardian angel may also help with getting into a calm and supportive mood. Experienced coaches suggest a minimum of 20 minutes to prepare before a coaching session.

Note that internal dialogue is a complex subject and internal reflection is a critical aspect to consider when deciding where to go next in the coaching session. This is a huge topic and this book merely brings its importance to the surface. Work on remaining neutral and focused during your coaching sessions with your clients. I strongly suggest you consult with your supervisor if your internal dialogue is intense and recurring.

64. What else should I watch for during a coaching session?

Not all the information the client gives you relies only on what is being verbalised. There are plenty of clues to explore, such as:

- Posture;
- Body language;
- Facial expressions;
- Hand gestures;
- Metaphors used;
- Eye movement;
- Voice tone;
- Hesitations;
- Energy levels.

The way the client is sitting offers significant insight into the way he is feeling or how his character is built. A hunched back and lack of smile can hint tiredness and apathy. Sitting straight and even leaning forward a little bit may reveal interest as well as willpower. Several approaches in the coaching world are based mainly on observing the client's posture and playing it back to him. It triggers thoughts. Sometimes naming 'the elephant in the room' helps the client become unstuck.

Body language is a good source of information during a coaching session. However, some can be easily misinterpreted. For instance, arms crossed may be interpreted as anger or defensiveness and may give you the wrong impression. Sometimes the person is cold or just needs reassurance and comfort. Playing back to the client what you see from their body language is a good way to break thinking patterns and to steer the conversation in other directions.

Facial expressions bear tons of information. From frowns and eyebrow movements to smiles and blank expressions, there is a significant amount of information. It often happens that coaches fear misinterpreting a client's expression and therefore retreat from mentioning it. The important thing is not your own interpretation (and, I can assure you, if your interpretation is incorrect the client will tell you), but rather the challenge and the client's own interpretation of what you are observing. You can simply ask "What's the meaning of the frown I am looking at right now?"

Fidgeting with the hands or other objects or merely *talking with the hands* can signal insecurity, nervousness, anxiety or furtiveness. As with the previous elements, observing fidgeting and playing it back to the client is fundamental to bringing his attention back to the here and now.

The use of metaphors is widespread and you will find them easily, in any type of conversation. Whenever we compare one thing to another, such as comparing a feeling to something else, we are using a metaphor. As Wendy Sullivan and Judy Rees explain in their *Clean Language* book, *"metaphoric thought and metaphoric language go hand in hand".*

Examples of metaphors are everywhere and exist in every language. "My relationship is on the rocks", "It's like walking on egg shells", "It's like talking to a brick wall" and "It's like a butterfly in my stomach" are all metaphors describing the way your client is feeling.

Exploring metaphors is a very powerful tool and doesn't require a load of questions. A simple, "Tell me more about it," or "Is there anything else about X?[9]" will trigger reflection and the client will be willing to share his thoughts and feelings.

Sensory acuity is the process of observing physiology. This includes watching eye movements, which can provide considerable insight as to whether the person is a visual, auditory or kinaesthetic person. A visual person thinks in pictures, so when they reflect upon a topic, they tend to imagine the final result and how it will look. You will find these individuals tend to slightly tilt their head backwards and look up, when answering questions. On the other hand, for an auditory person, who thinks in sounds, an eye movement to the side is quite common, as if they are hearing something. Finally, kinaesthetic persons would look down in order to be better connected with their feelings and not to have any type of distraction from the environment around them.

Voice tone is another great source of information. Notice pitch, intonation, volume and pace. All of these elements carry other non-verbal cues worth paying attention to. Usually when someone speaks a notch higher or faster it reveals nervousness or uncomfortable sensations. Speaking at a lower volume may signify embarrassment, secrecy or simply a feeling of fragility. Intonation carries with it a load of feelings, such as irritation, frustration, sadness, excitement and joy. Remember, these are only examples. It is advisable to be cautious with generalisations when talking to clients.

Hesitation before giving an answer may show confusion, uncertainty or even a lack of commitment. Picking up on these nuances can help the client be open about what really is going through his mind. A reminder that he or she is in a safe environment and can trust you often provides enough reassurance to less confident individuals.

Energy levels are a recognisable source of information that is difficult to ignore. When the client is very sad or overly excited it is easy to pick up on these feelings and refer them back to him. However, in situations where energy levels are not extreme it is harder to pinpoint and interpret. Nonetheless, the use of your own intuition will play a fundamental part in bringing the appropriate response to the client's behaviour, gestures, words or even silence.

---

9. This is a closed question. However within the *Clean Language* methodology, this type of question is part of a set of development questions that can be asked to help the client explore his own metaphor, without having the coach adding any of his own words. For further reading on Clean Language please visit www.cleanlanguage.co.uk

65. How can I build rapport with my clients without mimicking them?

You can build rapport in three main communication ways: body language (which is said to represent 55% of communication), voice tonality (38% of communication) and words (only 7%).

Within the body language field, a coach can always consider the mirroring and matching techniques. When mirroring someone you adapt their gestures and postures as if you were their image reflected in a mirror. If the client holds a glass of wine with his left hand you would hold the glass with your right hand. Matching is about doing exactly the same gestures and postures as the other person. Use these techniques subtly, so it does not appear you are mocking the client.

Another way of building rapport is through voice tonality, volume, pace and intonation. Beware of imitating someone's accent as this may be annoying to them.

Adapting the same energy levels can also create a good bond between two people. If someone is very excited and joyful matching their feelings will definitely create a bridge in your relationship. Even though opposites attract, in this situation that won't happen. If a person is feeling rather sad and meets someone else who is overly happy, the first impression may be that this person doesn't understand him or her and their first reaction may be to withdraw from their presence. Therefore neutralising or equalising your mood towards your client is a good starting point to building rapport.

The use of words can be effective even though words account for only 7% of communication. Different people use and prefer different communication channels. People tend to choose words depending on whether they are a visual, auditory or kinaesthetic person. If you listen to the kind of words used, they provide an indication of whether the person thinks in pictures, sounds or feelings.

Here is a short list of common words in all three channels:

Visual	Auditory	Kinaesthetic
Picture	Tune	Touch
See	Note	Grasp
Imagine	Accent	Impact
Look	Ring	Grab
Focus	Hear	Flat
Perspective	Key	Carry
Image	Harmony	Handle
Clarity	Voice	Throw
Define	Compose	Steer
Expose	Alarm	Hit
Illustrate	Speech	Move
Distinguish	Say	Smash

Matching preferred communication channels will definitely create a sound bond without mimicking. In particular, building upon the metaphors used by the speaker and using their language and vocabulary can be highly effective.

It's important to monitor the intensity you apply. In rapport building your judgement will play a key role in assessing how to build bonds with your client.

66. When is the right time to terminate the coach-client relationship?

Sometimes it is advisable to terminate the coaching relationship with your client. It takes strength, honesty and willpower to terminate the relationship. While that income source will cease, sticking to your coaching ethics brings peace.

Reasons why a client relationship might terminate include:

- When the coach becomes dependent on the client;
- When the client becomes dependent on the coach;
- When your coaching abilities are affected by illness;
- Conflicts of interest (emotional, financial, sexual, etc.);
- When other support, such as therapy, is more appropriate;
- When the client never makes, or ceases to make, progress.

Sometimes a coach will prolong the coaching engagement long after the time for termination has arrived. Dependency blurs the coach's judgement and negatively influences their ability to ask pertinent questions and to truly help the client.

The opposite case of dependency, when client is dependent on the coach, is more common. The individual feels he can't survive without the coach's support and therefore arranges discussions about endless topics that pose no real challenge.

A good coach knows when it is time to end the relationship. Breaking the pattern of dependency is hard and may take a few sessions, perhaps agreeing upfront that session X will be the last one.

In case of physical or mental illness, you may have to temporarily or permanently stop coaching. If you don't feel good about yourself then you may unconsciously transfer this feeling to your client. This is the number one action to avoid in a coaching relationship. Being ill affects your ability to self-manage, as well as to manage coaching sessions. It is not fair for the client who pays for the services of a healthy 'whole' coach.

In any circumstance where conflict of interest exists, end the coaching relationship. A conflict of interest is when one's impartiality, judgements and opinions are distorted by self-interest. As a professional coach you must be clear when you have crossed that line and be open about it. Some coaches prefer to refer the client to another coach, giving reasons other than the conflict of interest.

Finally, when your client doesn't seem committed and repeatedly makes no progress, one of the options is to finish the relationship, as the time you spend with this client could be better used helping someone else who is more committed to their goals. Another option is to be frank with your client and say you are concerned with his lack of commitment and progress. This conversation may well be his turning point.

In summary, ending a coaching relationship is about remaining honest and frank in terms of your abilities to coach and help your client with your coaching skills.

67. How can I ensure the best outcome for a coaching session?

No one can predict how a coaching session will end, what type of actions the client will decide to take or what the next steps will be.

But before we explore it further, what exactly is the best outcome? A to-do list, an action plan, a feeling of comfort, an energy boost? Who decides what the best outcome is? From personal experience, even though the coach facilitates the journey, the opinion of the client regarding what he has gained from the session will determine whether the client has been helped to achieve the best possible outcome.

There is a school of thought that says the best outcome is reached by matching the client's goal with suitable solutions to which the client can commit. Another school argues that the best outcome is to exceed the client's expectations and to supersede his objectives.

Nevertheless, both schools of thoughts would agree that what ensures the best possible outcome lies in excellent coaching skills - especially active listening and intuition, in reading between the lines and in getting information not verbalised by the client.

Expressing intuition and challenging the client to the point of reflection can only be effective in a relationship of trust where rapport is at its peak. Then the client is more serious about listening to your interventions.

Again keeping the client at the centre of the coaching session is key to a successful session. Focussing on the client, his issues, challenging him to think outside of the box and also acting as a mirror, so he can see how he comes across to other people and what his impact on others is, will definitely be a good approach to achieving the best outcome.

Some topics cannot be tackled in one session and require a series of coaching meetings. This means the best outcome may not be visible in only one session. A useful method to assess session progress is to periodically ask the client "How is the session helping you?" Some clients will be shy about giving sincere feedback and you can read not only their words, but also the way they answer, hesitate and so on.

Despite the fact that a coaching session is centred on the client, the coach will have a sense of accomplishment by the end of the session. Exploring this feeling will grant you invaluable information about how you did and how you can improve in future sessions. Discussing it with a fellow coach, a supervisor or even your own coach is a good idea.

68. Where do you draw the line between client confidentiality and moral obligation?

This is a very important topic and also a grey area. As a coach you must respect the client's right to confidentiality and follow an appropriate code of ethics that has to include not disclosing any information to third parties. This information can include details on gender, contact numbers, profession, age, etc. In fact, coaching businesses are recommended to register with local ICO, Information Commissioner's Office, and to list what type of information they are holding about their clients.

Legal obligation must be fulfilled regardless of your business. If relevant information is revealed to you by the client that is a matter of national or international security, or if the client plans to harm himself or others, or if he shares details of criminal activity, by law you must act upon this information and in some cases disclose it to the relevant authorities.

In these cases there is a fine line between client confidentiality and moral obligation. You may need to cross it if the consequences of not disclosing could have a greater impact.

Mention this obligation explicitly in your coaching practice ethical code and share it with your clients. Here is an example to help you create your own rules about client confidentiality and moral obligation:

> *"Coaches respect the confidentiality and privacy of their clients, colleagues and others with whom they do business. Unless authorised, coaches do not use confidential information for personal use or the benefit of any third party. Coaches can disclose confidential information or personal data only when appropriate approval has been obtained and/or they are compelled to do so by legal, regulatory or professional requirements."*

If you decide to take action against a client who has revealed information you feel obliged to report:

1. Consult with an experienced supervisor;
2. Talk to the client directly;
3. Inform coaching regulation bodies;
4. Inform the police or any other local relevant authoritative body.

Informing the police should be your last choice after consulting other sources of support who can guide you on the best action to take.

If you don't act on your suspicions and a crime occurs, even if minor, this may bother your conscience and may affect the quality of your coaching.

69. What are the most empowering methods of changing limiting beliefs?

Limiting beliefs are one of the universe's darkest power sources. They prevent us from achieving our goals and dreams, and from reaching our full potential.

Coaching assists clients with replacing limiting beliefs by empowering them to attain personal and professional objectives.

The four most popular methods for replacing disempowering beliefs are:

- **Personal affirmations**
  For an affirmation to be effective, four rules must be followed:

  1. It must be positive;
  2. It must be personal;
  3. It must be in the present tense;
  4. One must <u>truly</u> believe in it.

  Examples of affirmations could be:

- I deserve a promotion;
- I am a successful published writer;
- I am a happy, confident head of department.

  Often combining the use of a personal affirmation with a trigger is a powerful association. A trigger is simply something you hear, see, feel or smell that immediately triggers the specific thought. Repetition is an important factor in the equation, as is visualisation. Imagining the affirmation in its full glory is in itself an energy boost and a motivator.

- **Reframing**
  When a client is held back by a limiting belief, raising his awareness towards it is a first step in the NLP reframing technique. Explore your coachees' feelings attached to negative beliefs, and where these feelings come from in their bodies.

  The next step is to identify the self-talk related to a specific belief, with the goal of changing the self-talk voice to something quieter, or even of distorting the voice and replacing it with something like *Mickey Mouse's* voice.

- **Pattern Breaking**
This NLP technique is used when the client is well aware his negative self-talk is in charge. In specific moments when the client feels most strongly affected by a limiting belief, break that pattern. The client can achieve this by his clapping hands, pinching himself, shaking his head, breathing deeply and singing - anything which diverts his attention elsewhere.

By doing so the energy is removed from the negative thinking, the pattern is broken and the client can choose other subjects to focus upon.

- **Questioning**
You can challenge a disempowering belief by using questions that get the client to think about the pain associated with the belief and what it costs him. That is probably one of the best methods of changing a limiting belief. The easier the client finds it to associate pain with his limiting belief, the faster he will let go of it.

Use questions to allow the belief to come out into the open. Get the client to feel financial or emotional pain associated with his belief. Then get him to think forward and reflect upon a more positive outcome.

It is said that the more we question a belief the more it is likely to change. However during probing coach and client must be sure it is worthwhile questioning a particular belief.

- **Ask for evidence**
Requesting that the client looks for evidence to back up the limiting belief is often enough to bring about a realisation that the belief is based on illogic grounds.

These practical methods and techniques have been used by many coaches, with a very high success rate.

70. How can I help clients define new beliefs?

This NLP exercise follows a step-by-step approach which can take a long time to give results. It encompasses four important steps. This tool is recommended for use when the client wants or needs to replace an old belief with a new one, associating an empowering experience with a 'trigger' that can be accessed anytime, anywhere.

Step 1 – Ask the client to describe his feelings during an empowering experience

Usually, using questions, such as "What do you feel / hear / see?" is useful to the client to involve them in the experience and to transport them to that situation emotionally and spiritually.

Step 2 – Break the pattern by asking an insignificant question

The insignificant question can be about something totally different and banal, like the weather. This will help take the client's attention from the experience and clear his mind for the next step. It should be a question rather than a comment, so he feels the need to answer rather than remain quiet.

Step 3 – Help the client identify a physical trigger

A physical trigger is much simpler to use than an emotional trigger and has no hidden facets. A physical trigger could be an object of easy access the client carries at all times, like a key holder, a picture or a pen. It should be something with which the client is not in constant contact, such a mobile phone or Blackberry. Some people purchase special little objects specifically because the object has no former emotions attached to it.

Step 4 – Encourage your client to go over that empowering belief once more

This time the client holds his physical trigger at the same moment, whilst describing all possible details about his empowering belief. This step needs to be repeated over and over again, until his mind unconsciously associates the belief with the trigger.

Once the exercise brings results the client can use this tool wherever they are, whenever they wish. No one needs to know the special meaning of the little object they carry with them.

Our minds are constantly performing similar exercises with different thoughts. Haven't you associated the smell of eucalyptus or wood with the safety of your grandparent's house or a specific tune with an old love? This is exactly what happens when couples have their special song in a romantic relationship. It tends to be a song they heard when an empowering experience occurred – the first kiss, first 'get back together', first dance, etc.

Following the same lines, this exercise tries to combine the power of a positive experience with something the client has easy access to. Unconsciously, the client's mind associates the two and it provides a powerful feeling which in turn creates a positive change.

The trick is to always associate an empowering belief with a positive thought and feeling. Obviously, the exercise also works for negative and harmful thoughts, but those are the ones we want to get rid off in our day-to-day routines rather than to reinforce.

71. What contributes to self-esteem?

Self-esteem is how much we value ourselves, and is crucial for the understanding of ourselves and others. Low self-esteem makes us less aware of inner resources and is expressed in the way we feel, think and behave. Typically, the feelings associated with low self-esteem are depression, unhappiness, insecurity, victimisation and feeling uptight. These are corroborated by thoughts like "I'm a failure", "I won't be accepted or liked", "I can't do it" or "I'm too old / fat for that", just to name a few. Combining these feelings and thoughts with behaviours that are judgmental, defensive, aggressive and fearful is a powerful recipe for a sad outcome.

Internal and external factors contribute to a person's self-esteem. The internal factors determine how a person reacts to a particular situation or event and what he or she chooses to believe. For instance, failure can cause some individuals to give up and others to feel motivated to try harder. Apparently Thomas Edison, the American inventor who developed the light bulb, tried 10,000 times until he succeeded. The way he reacted to the first 9,999 attempts and what he chose to believe about his ability and knowledge has had an enormous impact our society. Edison did not see 9,999 failures. He saw 9,999 successes because each attempt taught him something new and got him closer to his goal.

External factors which come from our surroundings can also influence one's self-esteem. An example is rejection from others. The rejection of our services, opinions, ideas and feelings contributes to how much we value ourselves. Notice that self-esteem is always a matter of intensity - all of us have some degree of self-esteem!

Having high self-esteem causes us to be generous towards others, resourceful, open to the unknown and to trying new things, to be creative at work, interested in nurturing relationships, having joy in life and an expanded capacity for happiness.

Coaching will encourage the coachee to live more consciously, live in the moment, be aware of everything and generate a state of mind appropriate for every single moment while thinking for himself. This will impact his internal perception of self worth and manage the level external contributions have in determining his self-esteem.

What you choose to believe can affect your self-esteem. Being comfortable with who you are and what you do is the key to raising your self-esteem. Thomas Carlyle once wrote *"The history of the world is but the biography of great men."* How did these great men react to adversity and what did they believe they were capable of? What did they choose to believe?

72. What methods can be used to overcome low self-esteem?

Self-esteem is a vital element of success. It is influenced by external and internal factors, but it depends on us to get it right. When someone has high self-esteem it greatly affects their behaviour. We become better equipped to cope with life's difficulties and to nurture relationships with those around us. In addition having high self-esteem expands our own capacity for happiness, giving us strength and a thicker skin for facing adversities.

Positive self-talk is a coaching technique used for building self esteem. This is extremely powerful, but to yield positive results it must be done well. The fact that it is also available 24 / 7, anywhere in the world, makes it the number one tool to use. Examples of positive self-talk are:

- I can do it!
- I have done it in the past!
- Once there or once done I will feel strong / released / happy / safe / better!

For positive self-talk to work well it requires an extra effort. This extra effort is linked to the belief behind the words being said. A genuine belief and an authentic conviction will dictate the success of its outcome. Notice that in the case of negative self-talk there is no need for this extra effort, as negative thoughts tend to spread and torture one faster when linked with low self-esteem.

Another effective method is to choose the right language for enhancing self-esteem. There are some words like "try" that create room for failure. Help your client to be compassionate when talking about or to himself. Allowing the same standards as when talking to others is difficult for people who tend to be harder on themselves.

Another trick for enhancing self-esteem through adequate language is to drop words that exaggerate, generalise, minimise and discount one's actions or successes. It's common to hear people say "What I did is nothing important. Anyone could do that." or "I never do anything right." Help the client use language that is specific, factual, true and reasonable. They will certainly benefit from this.

You can increase the client's self-esteem by asking him to describe his positive qualities and things he does well in their eyes and in the eyes of others. At first it may seem a bit awkward and with some people you will need to wait in silence for a long time before you get any sort of answer. Don't dismiss the question if after a few seconds your client is still silent. Persevere in that silence and wait for the answer, which I guarantee will come.

A common exercise used by many coaches is to ask the client to relive past moments when his self-esteem was heightened and to describe his feelings and attitudes and how he behaved in those moments. This will help him break the pattern of self-discount and negative self-talk.

Visualisation is another tool used for raising self-esteem. Assist the client to imagine himself with high self-esteem and help him to notice and explore his body language, words and the way he looks at people in that image.

Increasing self-esteem is one of the hardest things to do since it deals with historic past tendencies, parental education, paradigms and the way one sees the world. The best thing when tackling it is to take one step at a time and to celebrate every accomplishment. Sometimes the best way for a grown up to learn is to take baby steps.

73. What are the best ways to explore clients' metaphors?

Metaphors are 'gifts' a client provides during the coaching session. With skill you can help the client explore his metaphors and get a better understanding of how he sees the world.

There are two main methods of exploring the client's metaphors. One already mentioned is through the use of David Grove's clean questions. The second is to probe the individual about what other information the metaphor provides. Both are very powerful. Using clean questions prevents the coach from adding any of his own imagery into the metaphor used by the client. Examples of clean questions are[10]:

- And what kind of X is that X?
- And that's X like what?
- And is there a relationship between X and Y?
- And when X, what happens to Y?
- And what would X like to have happen?
- And does X have a size or shape?
- And is X (on the) inside or outside?
- And how do/will you know?

As you can see these clean questions add little or nothing of the coach's own language to the exercise. Sometimes the syntax of the questions can seem sterile and the process can be repetitive, but it is an effective tool. The 'and' at the beginning of each question is, for the authors, less judgmental than starting a question with 'so', which is very common and can lead the client to thinking the coach is drawing conclusions. 'And' acts as a continuation of the client's thinking process and gives him the impression the whole *"interaction is being conducted from their perspective"*.

The second powerful method comprises four guidelines:

1. Apply the client's language and gestures;
2. Explore time dimensions;
3. Develop the aspects of the metaphorical image;
4. Match the client's pace and rhythm.

When the client is explaining a situation using his own words, the most disruptive thing the coach can do is to start using his own language, changing the metaphor to something he, the

---

10. These questions were taken from *Clean Language* by Wendy Sullivan and Judy Rees.

coach, is more familiar with. Replaying what the client says using the client's words and, where appropriate, the client's gestures, is the most basic principle a coach can follow.

Notice that you don't really need to ask a question. A simple "Tell me more" is enough to trigger a development of the client's metaphor.

The coach can explore with the client what happened exactly before, during and after the metaphoric image was painted. Exploring time dimensions is very helpful because it can draw a parallel with the real world. Questions such as:

- "What happens just before (client's words)?"
- "What else is happening as you continue to (client's words)?"
- "What happens next after (client's words)?"

...are enough to explore its timeframe.

Further developing the characteristics of the client's metaphor is a very good way to assist the individual in understanding what it really means. Use of questions that start with What, Where, Who, are some of the tools the coach can use.

Matching the client's pace and rhythm is a step forward when building rapport, but also gives the support the client needs during his self-discovery. This is definitely one of those moments in the session where the coach should restrain himself from being ahead or behind the client and walk by his side, metaphorically speaking.

Below is a summary of the dos and don'ts for exploring metaphors with the client.

Dos

- Use the client's language during exploration;
- Explore time dimensions to understand what happened just before the event, during the event and after the event;
- Develop the metaphor's characteristics;
- Match the client's pace and rhythm.

Don'ts

- Make assumptions;
- Change the client's metaphor into one more familiar;
- Get ahead or behind the coachee when pacing the exploration of metaphors;
- Make fun (although humour can break a limiting belief hidden in the form of a metaphor).

The following dialogue showcases the application of these guidelines.

Example

Coachee – I feel like a boat at sea. I feel lost.

Coach – What type of boat?

Coachee – Like those caravels packed with sailor men.

Coach – Who are these sailors?

Coachee – My team members, I guess.

Coach – Tell me more about what you see.

Coachee – I see an island far away.

Coach – Whereabouts is the island?

Coachee – Approximately 50 miles.

Coach – What does the island represent?

Coachee – I suppose it represents a safe harbour, where I don't feel lost at sea. Help, safety.

Coach – What do you need to do to get to that island?

Coachee – I need to summon my crew and together create a plan to navigate these 50 miles in a safe way without damaging the boat or sparing lives.

Coach – What corresponds to these actions in your life at the moment?

Coachee – Exactly! I need to have a meeting with my team and plan how to reach our sales targets, without increasing any costs or firing anyone.

74. How effective is scaling?

Coaches often use a scale when asking the client to quantify their commitment, enthusiasm, intention and importance of a topic.

Normally, the scale goes from one to ten, with ten the highest point of the scale. Typically, the scale is used when the individual talks in subjective quantitative terms and uses words such as *very, not so much, a lot, plenty, less.* Objectifying these terms by plotting them on a scale shows, without any misinterpretations, the level to which the client is referring. This allows the coach to apply this tool during a session to give clients some perspective and to help them to objectify the way they express themselves.

Here are some examples:

- On a scale of one to ten, with ten the strongest, how clear are you on what we've agreed you will do?
- On a scale of one to ten, with ten the strongest, how committed are you to reaching this by X?
- On a scale of one to ten, with ten the strongest, how excited are you about taking these actions?
- On a scale of one to ten, with ten the strongest, how high is your enthusiasm for taking that step?
- On a scale of one to ten, with ten the strongest, how important is this goal for you?
- On a scale of one to ten, with ten the strongest, how strong is your commitment to taking that step?

When asked this type of questions the client is confronted with having to think or rethink how it really is for them and that alone triggers a different perspective on the subject. When it comes to simple mathematical terms, such as a scale, no one can go wrong - it's easy to understand the relevance of the highest figure and the reality of the lower ones.

When the answer is lower than a seven or an eight, the client is not very committed, enthused about or strongly motivated about what is being discussed. Asking, "Which one thing could you do to raise the score a point?" will keep the client in the flow and implicitly suggests there is at least one action that would strengthen progress in terms of commitment, enthusiasm, etc.

75. How can I improve my coaching skills?

There are several ways to improve your coaching skills. Below are suggestions for developing your skills further:

- Practise with your existing clients;
- Get pro-bono clients;
- Coach a fellow coach;
- Revise your own telephone coaching calls and go through your interventions;
- Read coaching magazines;
- Watch other coaches coach in real life events or videos;
- Use the coaching tools developed by other coaches;
- Network;
- Teach others;
- Attend courses;
- Facilitate workshops and seminars about coaching skills;
- Learn from specific feedback;
- Listen to your supervisor or mentor's suggestions;
- Research the topic.

This list is not exhaustive, but comprises a good balance between practical exercise and theory. It is important that you identify your learning style(s) and, based on that, direct your attention to the best ways to acquire the knowledge you seek (please refer to the answer to question 44, which covers learning styles).

Nevertheless, practising is a fundamental element of any type of learning process. As they say *"Practice makes perfect"*. By practising you will stretch your comfort zone and learn from your experience. Trying new things will help you assess which tools resonate with your coaching framework and which tools don't work for you. Sometimes you must give a particular technique a second chance.

Practise diversity means trying new things. We never know from where or whom we will learn an invaluable lesson. Be open-minded as you walk the road of continuous improvement.

76. What do you do with difficult clients?

What makes a client difficult? Being overwhelmed? Loneliness? Desperation? Irritation? Regardless of the cause, a good coach must know where to position himself on the personal development spectrum during a coaching session, as presented in diagram 3.

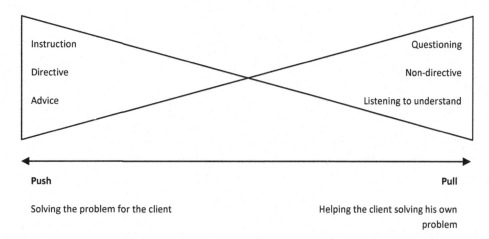

Diagram 3 – Personal development continuum

The advisory roles are directive and instructive. The client takes home some value from advice and feedback. On the other hand coaching is about safely raising the client's self-awareness to a point where he feels he can share his goals, fears and beliefs without judgement. Coaching offers support through appropriate levels of listening and challenging. It can improve the client's sense of responsibility for finding his own answers to his problems and for reflection.

Coaching can take many forms along this continuum and sometimes the coach can move back and forth to build trust and put the client at ease in order to bring him closer to his end goal.

The science behind dealing with someone who seems difficult is to assess the best remedy, taking into account individual characteristics. This is a difficult task in some cases, but this is where your skills as a coach come in – active listening and questioning, rapport building and intuition. You must read between the lines.

Note that clients draw their difficulties from both external circumstances and from limiting self-beliefs. When resistance persists they refuse either to be more aware or more responsible. They probably feel this will take them out of their comfort zone. John Whitmore, a world acknowledged coach, says the best approach is to apply high levels of patience and compassion and to be soft when questioning and challenging. However, in some situations clients respond well when provocatively challenged and when dark sides are exposed. Give them sufficient space to gather their thoughts. Exceptional preparation will enhance your intuition for managing these moments.

77. What safeguards must I take when coaching minors?

Coaching someone under 18 requires special consideration, mainly due to potential accusations of child abuse. Unfortunately, we are all aware of recent news about teachers, parents and caregivers who abuse children in schools, playgrounds, kindergartens and in their own homes. Therefore, when coaching a child, safeguards must be implemented:

- Obtain a CRB check[11];
- Have another coach co-facilitate the coaching session with you;
- Supervisory relationship with a senior coach;
- Requiring another adult to be present.

Before coaching, get written authorisation from the child's parents. It is essential that you report back to the parents on the progress achieved during the coaching session. Sharing your records (as previously agreed with the minor) is valuable and can help parents pursue a different approach at home or emphasise one already adopted.

When coaching someone under 18, be aware that your words may be taken as encouragement. Often, in their innocent view of the world, adolescents and young children don't evaluate all the consequences of their actions and reactions. Greatly influenced by the media, they believe some things can happen without any damage because they see it happen on TV. Who isn't aware of the six year old who threw himself out of the window thinking he had Batman powers? There are several stories like this one.

Coaching is very empowering, stirring a belief that everything is possible. However, be aware that children's minds are fertile soil and the development rate of new ideas in children is the fastest in the human race. When coaching a young child use your intuition to read between the lines and to guide the child to elaborate his answers without necessarily probing.

Coaching children also requires a good dose of patience. Children are known for being stubborn. Unlike adults children don't understand the necessity of pleasing others and going with the flow. So, don't lose your patience if you must repeat yourself countless times. Don't take things personally. Again, centre your practice around the client's feelings, not your own.

Do not become emotionally attached to the child as this may impact your coaching.

---

11. CRB check – check required by the Criminal Record Bureau to everyone who works with minors.

A similar situation happens when you believe the child requires more specialised support. Please refer the child to an expert. This is the case for any sexual and physical abuse and in extreme cases of bullying.

78. How can I express my intuition in a coaching session?

Intuition is what some call the 6th sense, a hunch for what is not being verbalised, heard or seen. Intuition is one of the must-have coaching skills. It can't be taught but once you discover yours you can develop it. The best way to enhance your intuition is to make use of it as much as possible. Some coaches suggest treating intuition as another dimension of information alongside observation.

You will know your intuition is working when the client's words, gestures and facial expressions don't match his verbal message. For instance, some people convince themselves they are telling the truth, but repetition, voice tone, hesitation, lack of eye contact and so forth prove to the careful observer that the whole truth is not being told. This feeling, this impression, is intuition. Frequently, people say "I am fine" as a polite answer to the common "How are you?" question, but the wooden response and lack of facial gesturing belies the answer.

Listening to intuition and acting upon it, by testing it out with the client, is a way of practising your intuition. Expressing one's intuition can be verbalised by saying "I'm sensing...", "My intuition is telling me that..." or "I get a sense that X is important for you". There are other, more provocative, ways, such as "Really?" or "I don't believe in that" that can land very well with clients. Notice that expressing your intuition typically comes as a normal sentence, an affirmation, which breaks the pattern of the questioning mode. It also must include the 'I', the fact that it's your intuition and not the truth. This gives you a lot of freedom and safety to experiment, because you are not pronouncing the reality but contributing your perspective.

Your judgement is key to assessing the situation and moving the case further. Some junior coaches tend to worry about whether they are interpreting the signs properly and whether their intervention is correct or not. Honestly, it doesn't matter whether the interpretation of your intuition is correct. What matters is the fact that expressing your intuition moves the client to action and deepens his/her learning.

After expressing your intuition as discussed above, it is quite common for the client to open up and share more information and details with you. However, bear in mind that answers such as "I don't want to talk about it" can also come your way. That may show your intuition was right. With an answer like that you can then address the subject from a different angle, always having the client's agenda in focus. Sometimes you must wait a while until you can return to the subject. That gives your client time to cool down and (re)consider opening up to you.

The trick when expressing your intuition is to keep quiet after your intervention and give space for the client to think and decide what and when to share with you.

79. What is self-coaching?

Self-coaching is nothing more than coaching yourself by applying the same skills and competencies as when you coach a client.

Self-coaching is basically switching on your self-talk to more useful ways to help you live the life you've always wanted. However, self-coaching is distinct from positive self-talk. Positive self-talk is about having a positive internal dialogue to help you boost your self-esteem and self-confidence and to grant you extra support in your daily tasks. Self-talk never exceeds the commentary level, whilst self-coaching is based on the challenge you pose yourself with powerful and pertinent questions, sometimes ones you don't want to answer.

Self-coaching involves a much deeper degree of sincerity than self-talk and the ability to answer questions you otherwise would never be confronted with. If you are very open and honest with yourself, self-coaching is a powerful tool for rethinking your strategies through the challenging and provocative questions you ask yourself.

Despite the fact that in self-coaching you only talk to yourself, it tends to work best when you speak aloud. It may sound a little bit crazy, but actually it is effective and helpful. Surely you talk to yourself, even if only to comment on every day things you notice about others, such as the colour of your friend's jacket, your neighbour's new hair style or the attractive looks of the stranger across the bar?

Your coaching skills must be excellent, especially your intuition and questioning skills. It isn't an effortless task. It takes plenty of perseverance and honesty to move forward with your answers. But I guarantee that your thinking process will be much clearer once you have gone through it.

On another note, self-coaching is far from self-recrimination and self-depreciation. You will need to avoid saying "I told you so" and other similar comments once you have answered your questions. When you play the coach's role, be aware of your voice tonality and intonation and try to be supportive and comprehensive.

Self-coaching is like being your own best friend. It is a support available to you at all times and only strives for your success. You can tap into this potential at any time. Try it! You will learn much more about yourself than you could ever imagine!

80. Who am I as a coach?

This is a fundamental question which requires an individual answer. Consider the following aspects: input, people and output.

Input is comprised of beliefs, values, personality, skills, competencies and abilities developed throughout life, the knowledge and understanding of the world gathered during the years, and work and life experience that shapes professional and personal life.

Beliefs coupled with core values are a powerful combination and, hopefully, a source of inspiration to many.

Authors such as Carole Pemberton and Mary Beth O'Neil mention the importance of signature presence in coaching. It is crucial to take time to reflect upon your signature presence, realising what you bring to the coaching relationship and what proves useful to the client through the coaching journey.

Coaching skills and abilities are something one can practise and develop over time. The technicalities of questioning and listening skills, expression of intuition, use of silence, paraphrasing and cultural awareness are competencies you may want to develop via appropriate coaching qualifications. Experiences drawn from previous professional environments will help you define who you are as a coach.

You may benefit by going through books you have read and reflecting on the various messages that have remained with you after reading.

People are also great influencers. Our experiences with people directly or indirectly cause paradigm shifts. Think of people in your life such as family members, friends, teachers, role models, bosses and neighbours, and reflect on how each has inspired you and educated you.

What type of people are you targeting in your practice? Dynamic, challenging, open minded and prejudice-free, interesting and good hearted individuals, who are tough when required but also friendly and inspiring, and who ultimately want to make a positive difference in their own lives and/or in the life of others? For some coaches, ideal clients are not afraid to try new things, are open to thinking 'outside the box', are willing to change and accept different methods and are, above all, hopeful. In contrast, consistently pessimistic people who are hopeless and avoid new things can be challenging and demand more from the coach's skills and competencies. Ultimately, if coaching delivers a positive change in someone's life, then the journey was worthwhile.

To properly answer the question "Who am I as a coach?" you must consider the coaching outcomes you hope to achieve with your clients. These can be reflection and increased self-awareness, inspiration and *aha!* Moments, action, positive change and belief in themselves.

On the other hand, as a coach, what do you hope to achieve in your practice? To be able to help someone to move forward in their thinking and fulfilment? To be inspiring and supportive? To live a more relaxed and healthier life style by achieving your own goals? To achieve a good annual income? To continue to develop as a coach with integrity and focus?

What would you describe as a positive outcome from a coaching engagement? The client's objectives (super)-achieved and goals reached? A*ha!* moments? The client's increase of self-awareness and clarity about life choices? Your sense of help and support? No feeling of being stuck, as a coach, during the coaching engagement? Feeling right about the way the coaching session(s) developed? Inner peace?

When coaching a client, review actions implemented at the beginning of each session by asking about the client's progress on the previous session's topic. In my opinion, the review of my own progress as a coach is best positioned at the end of each session, by simply asking the clients what has been gained or by explicitly requesting open feedback on my services. Nevertheless, the use of intuition and self-reflection, coupled with supervision support when required, will also grant invaluable feedback.

In summary, the question "Who am I as a coach?" can only be answered when you have reflected on the input, your influences, your desired audience and the outcomes you wish to achieve for yourself and your clients.

81. How do I coach?

Most coaches follow a pre-developed coaching model or their own coaching model.

To learn about existing coaching models, the Internet is a great source of information along with bookstores, libraries and your coaching support group.

The development of your chosen coaching model requires deep introspection.

A structured approach to the coaching process offers many advantages, particular if you prefer executive coaching. The executive client is accustomed to leaning on processes in order to feel comfortable managing assignments or projects. The junior coach is still building competencies in the field. Most coaching models are based on the GROW model or its most updated version TO GROW ME[12]. However, they are complemented with best practices drawn from various other models, such as the resourcefulness of the Coaching to Solutions model and the immediacy of Gestalt psychology.

Regardless of which model you follow, your session must be comprised of three main sections:

- **Contracting** – The beginning of the coaching engagement;
- **The main body** - Using the coaching framework to offer self-discovery and reflection;
- **The ending** – Summarising the session, action planning, reporting and feedback.

Contracting includes a focus on timing, highlighting the relevance of confidentiality and understanding the topic and its importance to the client. Sometimes coaches probe how the client will record the outcomes of the session. Recordkeeping can sometimes distract both client and coach, but can be a source of information for a later stage.

The main body of the session includes several phases:

- Client sets own goal for the session;
- Coach clarifies his understanding of it;
- Rapport and trust are built so the client feels safe to open up;
- Client shares his deepest fears about the realities and challenges he is attempting to sort out.

---

12. TO GROW ME is the latest version of the GROW model, which stands for Topic, Goal, Reality, Options, Way forward, Monitoring and Evaluation.

What your client does not say can be more telling than what he does say. As you gain more experience in the field noticing this will become a more evident skill. Silence allows the client space within which to answer at his own pace. For the coach, the client's reaction to silence carries a lot of information.

Helpful methods and techniques are based on extending without leading, encouraging without probing and reflecting back without interpreting. The immediacy of *here and now*, which can draw parallels with the *there and then*, can be as powerful as the use of pertinent questions. 'Dancing in the moment' and 'being in the moment', referred to by the Co-active Coaching model authors Whitworth, Kimsey House and Sandahl, will be essential for following the client's rhythm, pace and flow.

Personally, I believe in the power of asking the client to summarise the session at the end, rather than having the coach summarise it. This helps the coach understand relevant points, their order of appearance and the client's energy levels as he or she describes them. Checking for levels of commitment is another technique that proves useful, especially when associated with scaling. Please refer to question 74 for additional information.

Finishing the session in an energetic and clear tone will provide the client with proper motivation and a feeling of positive outcome and mission accomplished. The final moments will be to assess what the client has gained from the session and by doing so to get feedback from him, which will most likely spark improvement in your coaching in future sessions.

Note that this coaching process can be easily followed in a single session (beginning, middle and end), but also offers the flexibility for a full coaching engagement with six or more sessions.

Most coaching processes don't bring anything new to the existing collection of coaching models. Uniqueness lies in combining the model with your signature presence, the excellent use of the techniques learned and full focus on the client's experience and agenda.

82. What stretches me as a coach?

This is a very personal question. To answer honestly you must understand your comfort zone as a coach. In what areas of your coaching practice are you most comfortable? Is it in the model you apply? Or the skills you use? Is it in the type of coaching you offer, e.g. telephone coaching? Or in the exercises and techniques you apply in each session?

I am sure the list is long. But there are certain things you haven't tried yet - things that could enhance your practice or give it a new perspective. These could be a specific exercise, the use of materials like flipcharts and drawings or even different type of questions. Once someone has identified their learning style and their comfort zone it is quite common for them to stick to it.

However, I have news for you! You've got to get moving and stretch your comfort zone. If you don't, someone else will... and they are likely to take your client away from you.

So, how do you go about stretching your comfort zone as a coach? The first step is being prepared to stretch yourself personally as a coach. Be willing to learn new things at your own pace and have an open mind as to what comes. The second step is to identify in what direction your comfort zone needs stretching.

The following exercise, which I developed and do with my clients and fellow coaches, is called Comfort Zone's Spider Web. First identify your comfort zone areas. These may include skills, exercises, models or processes, use of materials, type of coaching (face-to-face, telephone, etc), techniques and methods. Please refer to diagram 4.

Assess yourself in each area using a scale one to ten, with ten the highest. Be truly honest in your self-assessment. After that plot your scores in a spider web diagram and look at the result.

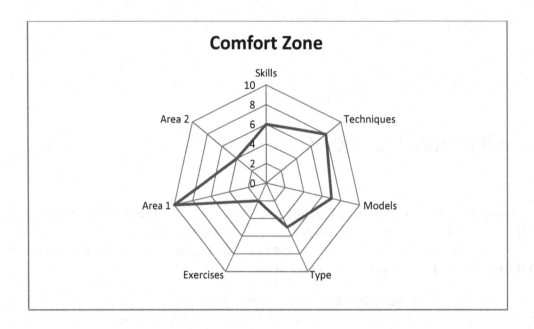

Diagram 4 – Comfort Zone's spider web

Ask yourself the following questions:

1. Where can I stretch my comfort zone?
2. What actions would increase my score in each subzone?
3. Which one area will I try first?
4. Who could help me?
5. Where can I learn more about this area?

This is a structured approach for identifying how to act on areas of weakness. Following your own pace has its advantages, as has being challenged by your own coach, mentor or supervisor. Consider discussing the results and answers to these questions with him or her.

Once you have researched, learned and practised new skills and techniques in a specific area, reassess yourself on the spider's web. Once you have completed this, prepare to take on the next challenge.

Another good way to assess yourself (besides honest self-evaluation) is to simply ask your clients and/or colleagues to provide specific feedback. Be aware that sometimes feedback can be inflated. Therefore the best way is to combine a 360 degree evaluation with your own self-assessment. Have a good stretch!

83. How can I become the best coach I possibly can?

Whether you have made coaching your main profession or not you must be truthful with yourself about your skills. The one person you must be totally honest with is yourself. When someone is authentic and open with themselves about their accomplishments and shortcomings, it is much easier to improve.

Some people like to brag about their good results and how things are going so well for them. But when the lights go off, a different truth may appear.

Being the best coach you can possibly be is linked with truthfulness and directness about your abilities. You won't need to be open about it with anyone else. Being open with yourself is sufficient. Once this is done you can move forward and choose how to close the gaps you have identified, or whom to contact for support or help with when to take action.

For procrastinators this is bad news. Procrastinators don't enjoy taking immediate action. However, for those driven by success and willpower, walking the extra mile to improve and enhance themselves as a professional and as a human being is a welcome exercise.

Note that being the best coach you can possibly be isn't linked with being the most successful and well paid coach of all time. Unfortunately the reality is that these two are not synonymous. However, being the best coach you can possibly be may open doors to success.

Coaching for Solutions, one of the most prominent models in the coaching industry, is based on the principle of resourcefulness, meaning that the individual has the answers within him. In addition it is always useful to have feedback from your clients and peers before you assess your skills. Following these thoughts, you will have the answers within you regarding what you still need to improve to become the best coach you can possibly be. The best way to tap into your resourcefulness is to turn down the 'noise' around you – other's opinions, mischievous comments from people around you, peer pressure, overwhelming feelings, etc. – Listen intently to your inner voice and it will show you the way. Don't confuse this inner voice with the 'saboteur voice', the one that is so full of itself that it spoils your self-esteem sooner or later.

You can always go back to your coach and bring the topic up in one of your regular meetings. He or she will assist you to think about options on how to become the best coach you can possibly be.

Part III – Tips for Growing Your Coaching Business

This section explores marketing techniques and ideas on how to grow your coaching business. Here are more details about common doubts, defining a coaching niche, marketing traps, coaching packages and offers, partnership and reducing costs. In addition I will discuss other products and services for diversifying your coaching business, and myths about setting coaching rates.

84. How can I define my coaching niche?

All coaching marketing literature prompts you to define your coaching niche as a first step in setting your business. This is one of the most important steps as it is a critical milestone in the path of building your practice. Deciding what type of coaching niche you will focus on dictates your target audience, vocabulary and terminology, etc., for building effective promotional materials and getting positive results fast.

Defining a coaching niche is a serious task and should not be taken lightly. Take your time to identify potential areas and to ponder the pros and cons for each approach.

Some ways to identify your niche are to think about your passions, ideals and dreams. From where do you draw inspiration? What makes you tick? This approach speaks directly to the dreamer in you and will release positive energy and motivation for accomplishing what you want. However, you may need to acquire certain skills and knowledge in order to fulfil the competencies required in that coaching niche. For example, if you want to become a dedicated coach within the weight loss arena several coaching schools now provide specific courses on niches such as this.

Another way to define your coaching niche is to identify where your expertise lies. In what areas do you have experience? What do you already know and do well? This is probably a more rational and methodical way of choosing a niche and it can help with the credibility issues associated with being a coach. A good example is executive coaching. Many senior managers have decided that, based on their executive board experience and their many years spent in dealing with companies and directors, they would like to use that knowledge by breaking into the coaching world as an executive coach.

How a coach should define his niche is an individual decision. Some make use of being coached through this process, with very interesting results. One of the most powerful tools is visualisation. This technique is simple enough to apply in self-coaching. Simply picture yourself in the future, coaching in a specific niche. Once your image is created try to identify how you feel and act, who is there with you, what you are saying, what your surroundings are, etc. If a specific niche is not ideal for you, you will know it - the visualisation will not resonate with you - you will experience feelings of discomfort during the exercise or you simply won't be able to see yourself in the niche. For additional support consider doing this activity with a coach.

The important thing is to really feel energised by the selected coaching niche. This is crucial since you will be spending a lot of time working in this area.

Obviously you can always change, add to, or adapt your coaching niche. However, the process is time-consuming and sometimes stressful. Marketing materials would require updating (website, business cards, promotional material, etc.) and a significant number of details would need to be thought through, such as your target audience and communication channels. Take your time to define your coaching niche.

85. Who could my clients be?

This question is very much connected with the previous one about the coaching niche. As soon as your coaching niche is defined you can easily identify your target clients. If you specialise in divorce coaching your clients are predominantly people who want to get divorced, are divorced, are in the process of getting divorced, or are perhaps even trying to avoid a divorce. Teaming your services up with divorce attorneys and lawyers may be a good starting point for boosting your practice, as well as for requesting referrals.

On the other hand if you specialise in business coaching for small and medium enterprises, picking up a Companies' House list or yellow pages could be step number one to finding more clients.

Some coaches say that defining the niche is the most difficult part of building a coaching practice and that getting clients is the easy bit. Let's assume you have already defined your niche. So, how would you go about getting clients? Regardless of the chosen niche there are three essential steps that will help coaches identifying where to find more clients:

1. **Search for associations, organisations and other companies to partner with** – Search where your target audience belongs, visits, socialises, reads, participates, etc.

2. **Meet them** – make sure you are visible to these people by attending and speaking in the networking events / conferences / workshops they attend and by writing articles for the magazines they read, etc.

3. **Get your credibility and name out there** – Interestingly enough, we often buy where our friends buy. So, if a friend of yours mentions a very interesting magazine to which he or she now subscribes, you tend to check it out. The same applies for services, namely coaching services. Tap into the circle of influence of paying clients. Ask them to refer you to their friends and contacts.

However, if you haven't yet done your homework on defining your niche, this doesn't mean you will not find any clients. Not at all! It just means your effort to find them may be greater as you will need to target more avenues to success.

There are some coaches who approach their coaching niche the other way around. First they identify what sort of people they like to work with and then they define their niche. The process starts by answering the following questions:

- **With what type of personalities do you work well?** – Reflect on personal traits, cultural backgrounds, styles, etc;

- **How would you describe your ideal client?** - Reflect upon their characteristics;

- **With what type of personalities would you not wish to work?** – Sometimes clearly identifying what we don't like is a way of identifying what we do like;

- **What personal traits that you can identify in others create the biggest challenges for you?**

- **What working environment suits you best?**

Reflecting upon your answers to these questions will provide a sense of your interactions with people, the challenges you face and the opportunities created when you work with people who bring out the best in you. This journey requires serious consideration. Take your time to tackle the issue from different perspectives, as if you were coaching one of your clients.

86. What are my clients looking for?

People come to coaching with the idea that something must change: their lives, themselves and/ or their behaviour. They are after something or someone who can ease their pain quickly. Clients are looking for answers, results, solutions and, due to time constraints, quick fixes.

All those answers, results, solutions and quick fixes are within the client. Your job, as a coach, is to bring them out, make the options clearer to the client and to help them prioritise, choose and take action.

Some clients are also seeking advice, words of encouragement and support. Whilst the coach must assess where the client falls in the coaching spectrum (please refer to the diagram in question 76) the coach should never tell the client *what to do*. Instead, the coach should gently guide the client to his own conclusion. Giving your own opinion as a human being is very easy — we are taught to do this throughout our lives, when the media constantly bombard us with "What would you do?" type situations. But in a coaching environment you must focus on the client's agenda and restrain yourself from answering that type of question when your client asks you.

Answering a client's question, such as "What would you do in my place?", can be somehow taken by your coachee as the right answer. Unconsciously they tend to follow it, even when it doesn't resonate with their personality and their vision.

According to Dr. Robert Cialdini, who conducted thorough research on persuasion, one of the six "weapons of influence" (or principles of persuasion) is authority. People follow authority and in a coaching environment your client somehow identifies you as the authority - just as in school when pupils view the teacher as the authority or on the street with policemen.

The risk in taking the easiest way out (answering your client's question) is that it might appear to imply that your client should do what you think is right. Some clients are in very dark places when they come to coaching and may blindly follow your answer without reflecting upon the consequences and challenges they would face in their situation.

A way to escape from answering questions is to ask another question or simply to remind the client that the focus of the conversation is on them, not on you. This does not need to be confrontational. In fact in this part of the conversation you should use a supportive voice tone and not a condescending one.

By challenging the client you help him to find the answers, results and solutions he needs. Sometimes the answers to his problems aren't clear right away and he may feel overwhelmed with more questions, challenges and the need for more reflection, to the point of frustration or irritation. You must assess when to challenge and how to challenge. This is where your skills and presence play a vital role in distinguishing yourself from your fellow coaches.

The quick fix offered by answering a client's question may seem worthwhile but may only have temporary value. Assist the client to search more deeply for a more solid and robust solution to their problem. Everything is a matter of time and effort. What they do next and how they proceed is their choice and not yours. If that somehow affects the quality of your coaching then it is highly advisable that you seek supervision or simply cease coaching the client.

However, in some cases the client is so lost within himself that he cannot make a decision. In these situations, you must question if coaching is actually the right type of support and if a different kind of help might be more suitable for your client.

87. Which are the best strategies for creating my coaching profile?

A coaching profile is a summary of your coaching experience, models and skills. It gives the reader a sense of who you are and how you coach. It should be written in such a way that the reader feels compelled to get to know you at a deeper level and to learn more from you. It should be inspirational, to the point and give enough information without being too extensive.

A coaching profile isn't the same as your CV. It should provide sufficient data about you as a coach in three to four paragraphs. One way to build your coaching profile is to base it on your CV and to extract the parts that are most important.

A coaching profile can include:

- Qualities as a coach;
- Previous relevant experience within or outside the coaching field;
- Credentials, qualifications and accreditations;
- Your picture;
- What's in it for the prospect;
- Information about your coaching model(s).

Another good strategy for building your coaching profile is to go through previous feedback forms and appraisal evaluations from previous employers to select some feedback. This feedback tends to be specific and straightforward and can add to the value of your coaching profile without making it too long.

A third strategy is to create a profile based on testimonials from previous clients. If you are new to the business, offer your coaching services to a few acquaintances and friends and ask for their honest feedback. Select the phrases that best resonate with you and your way of coaching and use them to create your profile.

It is also useful to include some reflections on how you want to coach, how you would like your coaching to be perceived and how your clients feel during and after a coaching session.

Your profile should include information about your experience in the world of coaching and any other relevant experience. Many coaches include accreditations and prominent clients.

Don't forget to include some wording conveying what you bring to your client, i.e., what are the benefits of your service to a client? Your unique features such as specialisations, linguistic skills and proven techniques are useful additions that can match prospect demands.

You may create several profiles to suit different markets. Highlight distinct attributes in each to speak your audience's language. Always be honest and convincing.

88. What are the best techniques for finding new coaching clients?

Growing your coaching business has nothing to do with pure luck, but is about perseverance and continually trying new things. Obviously, being the right person in the right place at the right time can play a role in the process.

The list below isn't exhaustive, but it includes suggestions on how to find new clients. Not all of them will bring you clients though these ideas are considered by many coaches to be the most successful techniques:

- Network with participants in coaching events;
- Cold calls to individuals and/or corporate companies;
- Associate with coaching services companies;
- Enrol with coaching associations;
- Explore your local business area;
- Lead a local coaching support group;
- Give a few sessions on a pro-bono basis;
- Tap into your own personal network of acquaintances;
- Contact previous employers and colleagues;
- Distribute free products to a circle of people in exchange for their contact details;
- Attend networking events;
- Write press releases about your work;
- Promote your business through various means of communication (online, radio, newspapers, etc);
- Offer referral promotions to existing clients.

Attending a coaching event or any other related event is one of the best ways to meet people who are interested in coaching and/or are looking for a coach. Sharing your experience as a coach and using your interpersonal skills creates a bond with them. This can be explored at a later stage either by becoming a mentor/supervisor to them or coaching them.

Many coaches develop a script to use on telephone calls when contacting new prospects to promote their services and this often ends up with a contract. Although cold calling can be tedious and you may find it difficult to reach the person you wish to speak to, it can also grant you good results. You will need to find out whether it works for you.

Becoming an associate with coaching services providers or becoming a member of any coaching association gives access to their coaches' directory where contact details and profiles can be seen by anyone who accesses those sites. Keep your CV or *résumé* updated at all times!

There are lots of opportunities in your local area. Introduce your practice to other businesses and increase your exposure to your local community by leading a coaching support group. Often people who are interested in coaching will attend the regular meetings and will quite likely want to talk to you about their issues and what type of coaching you offer.

A good starting point for finding new clients is to explore the networks of your personal acquaintances and friends. They may work for companies which could benefit from coaching or they may know people who need coaches. Even though your network may already be a good size, expand it by tapping into your friends' networks. Don't waste this opportunity by being shy or afraid of what others may think. It may well turn out to be positive for everyone.

Your previous employer and ex-colleagues are other possible sources of new clients. They know your strengths and your skills and will definitely help you if they feel there is a win-win situation. You will only know once you have tried it.

One of the most popular techniques in modern marketing is to give something for free in exchange for contact details. It is common to see ads for free newsletters, DVDs, reports, etc., on the Internet. The person signs up and thus gives permission to receive the freebie by sharing their contact details. This is the beginning of a relationship which can bear fruit in the future.

Attending networking events is a good way to find clients. However, be smart when choosing which events to attend. There are plenty of events where you will meet other coaches with similar intentions and that may dilute your impact on prospects.

Promoting your business by writing press releases, giving interviews to local newspapers and magazines or appearing as a guest speaker on a radio show are other effective techniques for becoming known. Perhaps when someone reads the article or listens to the radio programme your words will help them. Other examples include creating your own flyers, advertising in phone directories (which could be free of charge), e-zines and direct mail.

Finally, offering your clients a free session when they refer a new customer increases your client base.

With all of these options the point is to sell your services and your qualities as best as you can. There is no need for lies or exaggeration. Simply convey the message about how your services will help someone to move forward. Most definitely there is a demand for your services, so wherever you are be clever in matching your offering to the demand. Soon you will be profiting from it.

There are some coaches who offer promotions on the basis of, 'your money back guaranteed'. Whilst this may seem a bit too 'selly', it conveys a message that the coach feels very confident about his or her services.

In the end it's all about how you are perceived!

89. How can I promote my coaching business?

Promoting a coaching business is very important when you are starting out and it is often overlooked. Even if you already have paying clients, promoting your business is a regular task that should be on your to do list all the time.

Here are top eleven tips for promoting your business:

1. **Word of mouth** – Ask current clients to recommend you or refer you to their acquaintances and friends. This is the most cost effective promotional method since it costs nothing. You may consider giving business cards to your friends for them to give to people who may be interested in your services;

2. **Networking and following up on new contacts** – The best way to showcase your skills is to be yourself and to let others experience a little bit of you. Therefore attending networking events is a must. Pick one or two per week and make every effort to attend. There are several bodies and associations you can link to which organise these events on a regular basis. Show up with your best smile and a stack of updated business cards. After you collect people's cards, make sure to put their details on your contact database. Every now and then drop them a line and let them know your latest business news;

3. **Direct Mail and follow up** – Create a simple information pack with a cover letter, brochure, testimonials from previous clients and press releases about coaching. Ideally these would be written by you or about you / your work. If that is not possible yet, research interesting press releases about coaching (not about a specific coach in particular) and let your recipient read about the wonders of coaching. That works as a teaser and the results can be very positive. A few weeks after you send the pack, follow up with a short call. Be spontaneous on the call and don't pressure the person to read your information pack. Rather, draw their attention to a specific area you want to highlight, such as your offers or a certain paragraph of your cover letter.

4. **Press releases** – For some of us reading our names in print is a thrill. It spreads the word about your achievements and your work. If you aren't comfortable writing articles, ask one of your friends or search for a freelance writer online. Get the word out about your work on a local radio station, in local newspapers and libraries, on blogs and online forums and in e-zines. You can leave copies of your articles in public libraries, hairdressers and on notice boards, etc. Make sure you distribute them in places where your target audience goes and socialises. Position yourself as an expert in that field and soon you will

get replies. And don't forget websites, such as *PRweb*, a press release online distribution service;

5. **Joint-ventures** – Consider who has access to the people you want to reach. Some coaches create "partnerships" with other professionals and facilities, such as massages centres, nutrition centres and the Chamber of Commerce, to benefit from their list of contacts;

6. **Website** – Create your own website where updated information about your services, yourself, testimonials, etc., is available 24 hours a day. You can create a free report about an interesting topic related to coaching which viewers can download for free in exchange for their contact details. Research the best prices for web design services and ensure the free report you give out is interesting to your target audience. In addition, investing in search engine optimisation (SEO) may be of interest, in order to position your webpage higher in the ranking searches. Search online for SEO companies and quotes;

7. **Personal emailing** – The days of impersonal mass emails are over. Customers like to be treated individually. You can purchase automated emailing systems and send periodic personalised emails to your contact list, without the need do it manually. There are several companies which specialise in this field. Search for them online. *ConstantContact*, *Aweber* and *MyEmma* are well-known providers. Ensure that you communicate clearly in all the emails and newsletters you send. Make it punchy and lean. People don't want to be bombarded with long emails. The trick is to keep your audience interested in you and what you offer;

8. **Up-selling** – at the precise moment a client is purchasing one of your products / services / packages, you can offer them an additional sale presenting them with a bigger, more expensive package which is perceived as better value for money;

9. **Increase cost of services** – Some practitioners have different price lists depending on who is buying (disguised as different services). Whilst that may be considered unethical, there is nothing that prevents you from increasing the cost of your services the second time round. Make sure you communicate this properly and explain that your rates will be increased by x% once the package comes to an end. If the coaching relationship is strong and the increment is not exaggerated, many will be the clients who remain loyal to you;

10. **Diversify your products and services** – If you are currently only selling coaching hours, consider selling workshops, speeches, reports and combined packages, etc;

11. **Create a blog or newsletter** – Where you share updated articles and thoughts with your public.

There are plenty of other interesting suggestions you can apply. I recommend that you read through marketing articles and books or attend one of the hundreds of seminars about how to boost your business.

90. What are the most common marketing traps for coaching businesses?

My first thoughts go to advertising. Misconceived advertising can empty your pockets and may not yield many results.

Advertising doesn't need to be in the form of an ad in a magazine or newspaper. Phone and contact directories, such as the yellow pages, are another way to spend money without seeing many returns. Be wary of their promise of a high number of visitors to your homepage for a monthly fee. Whilst traffic may come nothing guarantees visitors will buy from you.

In essence, advertising works only when you target your particular audience correctly. Including an ad in your local telephone directory and expecting the CEO of an international company to contact you about your services may be fruitless. To be successful you first must identify your market and then evaluate which advertising strategies are likely to be most effective.

A second marketing trap is relying on only one or two marketing strategies. There are plenty of marketing strategies that can help grow your business. These are referrals, telemarketing, joint-ventures, direct email, leaflets and brochures, events and exhibitions, the Internet and search engine optimisation, to name just a few. Expand your marketing plan by including several different strategies. Chris Cardell, a well-known Marketing specialist, advises businesses to use ten to twelve different marketing strategies.

The third misconception is to apply every strategy to the whole of your circle at once. First test your marketing plan on a small scale and only risk what you can lose. If it doesn't work, stop it; if it works, then roll it out. You can test different wording and letter styles: you can test changes to your website: test distinct headlines and also test different prices.

The fourth marketing trap according to Chris Cardell relates to the marketing budget. His advice is to drop the concept altogether and instead decide how much you are willing to pay for each new client. There are different levels of expenditure for each new client and different strategies. Decide which one is best and go for it. To do this, you must evaluate the average long-term value of each customer.

Another common trap for coaching businesses is failing to maintain a steady stream of referrals. Coaches work with existing clients and neglect to expand the practice by exploring other markets. Don't limit yourself to what you do now. Stretch your comfort zone and open yourself to new opportunities, new products and services.

Finally, the darkest of the traps is related to your mindset. Break free of the idea that marketing has nothing to do with you and that you aren't good at it. Someone once said, *"Your attitude almost always dictates your altitude in life."* Be positive and embrace marketing as the vehicle for a profitable business. Just the paradigm shift alone will open new doors.

91. What are the most common coaching packages and offers?

Very often new coaches restrict their services to coaching hours and their fees to the amount that can be reasonably charged for a one-hour session. Whilst there is some value in doing this, a more experienced coach aware of market demands might create monthly fees or package fees to break the client's connection between one hour of coaching and a specific hourly fee.

If you allow your clients to fall into the mindset of 'fee for service', it will be much more difficult to move them to another level and to move your business forward with new revenue streams.

In our society people tend to simplify things and to equate time with money. Additionally, there is a subconscious principle that everything perceived as cheap has no value. Thus when pricing a coaching session many coaches lower rates below those of their competitors, hoping to gain more clients. This strategy will not work as expected, since customers are often willing to pay more for a perceived 'expert' rather than pay less for services of inferior quality.

When devising your pricing strategy, take into account your target audience. What are they willing to pay? How do they perceive value versus cost? What type of packages would they be interested in?

It is common practice to sell packages of six to ten life coaching sessions purchased together. Some coaches offer one or two sessions for free. However, executive clients are more interested in benefits beyond the session itself and proof of the value they will receive overall. Hence, executive coaches like to work on monthly packages, the number of sessions depending on urgency. For instance, if the businessman needs to reach his objective in three months, fortnightly sessions for a minimum of three months may interest them. The time in between sessions is reasonable enough to show progress, without adding to the overwhelming weekly agenda of most executives. These packages also include unlimited email support, a certain number of telephone coaching sessions and/or other types of support, such as team coaching or teleclasses on various topics.

Search within your niche to uncover what your competitors are doing and what clients expect. With this knowledge you can adapt your offering, adding your own personal touch and signature to differentiate your services from those of your competitors.

In summary, sell your customers what they want. You can only do this when you truly know your customers. Test your marketing and pricing strategies with your supervisor or mentor, or even friends, and adapt as necessary. You will only know if it works when you try it!

92. What other services can I offer apart from coaching sessions?

Coaches sell their time. This can leave little room for creative thinking. Yet to survive you must be creative. Some coaches have found great success by continuously reinventing themselves and selling many types of related information products. In fact, they have so cleverly developed their sales strategy that coaching sessions are likely to be their smallest source of income.

Coaching is a service profession. There is no tangible product sold. Coaches dedicate time to listen to clients and, in a supportive and challenging way, to help clients find their own solutions to life's problems.

This is the core of your coaching business, but you can also branch out to provide products to your customers, such as books, audio CDs, workshops, reports, mastermind classes, etc. These may be your own products or you may sell appropriate products created by other coaches.

This marketing 'funnel' shows how both coaching and products can impact your coaching business.

Diagram 5 – The Marketing funnel applied to Coaching businesses

As one progresses deeper and deeper into this marketing funnel, the cost of investment to the client increases, as well as the selection of clients who are willing to pay. One method for slowly enticing customers to pay for products and services is the up-sell. The up-sell process, when done correctly, is beneficial for the client as additional more advanced resources, not available at the free level, become available for a fee.

> **One Up-sell Example**
>
> Mary has been visiting a coaching website for several months, downloading free reports and other resources. The website owner, an experienced coach, can see that Mary has become a good customer, albeit a free one. The coach, Susan, wants to communicate at a deeper level with Mary, so she writes to offer Mary one free coaching session. Susan's email praises Mary for her sincere attempts at self-development and offers a list of additional benefits Mary will receive through one-to-one coaching. Mary is thrilled to receive personal attention from Susan, accepts the offer and within a month is paying Susan's full price for coaching services. Susan, effectively, up-sold Mary from zero income to becoming a regular paying client.

There are hundreds of ways to up-sell to your clients. Be creative.

Public speaking is an excellent tool for broadening your visibility among potential clients. Not everyone is comfortable with public speaking. If this describes you, you can avoid speaking in public and still get your message across. Record an audio CD, a series of teleclasses or a webinar, which allows you to go at your own pace. Begin by recording your coaching sessions with a client, which can be done quite easily by Skype. Get permission from your client or anyone else you are speaking to before recording the call. A potential client can go through the session in their own time. After you become more relaxed about creating these presentations, choose a topic you enjoy and brainstorm ideas on tackling the topic from a different angle. What alternate perspective might you offer to potential listeners? What challenge is worrying your prospects... and how can you help them reach their solutions? Can you brighten someone else's day with your unique brand of wisdom?

Creating information products over the internet is nearly hassle-free. Most recordings can be saved as Mp3 audio files, meaning you can simply email the recording to others or to a downloadable link with no need to burn a CD or DVD.

Once you feel more comfortable with public speaking, develop a brief workshop on a specific 'hot' topic and provide your services as a guest speaker to various appropriate organisations. Starting on a smaller scale will give you the strength and confidence required to tackle bigger crowds. You will learn from your inevitable mistakes on a smaller scale and can apply these learnings as you reach bigger audiences.

No matter which methods you choose, don't forget what coaching is all about. The marketing jungle can confuse your main coaching purpose, especially if you begin to see dollar figures everywhere. The core of coaching is about helping the client find his own way. It is too easy to start making suggestions, leading the client into ways you believe are simpler and faster. You need to remain true to coaching, and to restrain yourself from being judgmental and/or directional. This will apply in all the services you provide as well as the products. So, when you give a workshop or a teleclass about coaching, have your coach cap on, and excel in this rewarding profession of helping the maestro (the client) conduct his own orchestra (his life).

93. Who can help me grow my business?

There is plenty of help available to assist you in growing your coaching business. Before you can determine the type of help you need, some introspection is necessary. Do you require emotional or motivational help? Financial support? Marketing ideas? Being specific about the type of help you need is the starting point.

Emotional support can be found among friends and family members, but you may also want to rely upon a sound coaching network where you can bounce ideas around and learn from others' experiences, successes and difficulties. Your coach is an excellent source of emotional help when growing your business.

Financial assistance might come from banks, investors and fund management companies willing to advance funds to get you started. Coaching is one of the few professions where investment is kept to the minimum, since the only requirements for starting a coaching practice are associated with accreditation and typical business expenses, such as phone bills, Internet access and travelling expenses. Additionally, grants from institutions and government entities can provide financial support.

Motivational help can be found by reading motivational and self-help books, attending seminars presented by motivational speakers and watching inspirational movies. Motivation is an element that must be linked with structured thinking and action planning in order to grant fruitful results.

In the modern world there are many people and companies whose main objective is to help you market your business. Often free membership is provided for several months. You may be entitled to teleclasses, webinars, informational reports, DVDs and other resources focusing on creating a profitable business. Some programmes are operated by unscrupulous individuals who want to take advantage of your need and your trusting nature. Always trust your intuition and your first impression of the company. Research the company online and never give your money to any online or offline companies who cannot provide solid business references.

Joint-ventures (JV) are another way to grow your business. Unlike a partnership, which is a legal entity, the joint-venture gives you access to someone else's network and pool of contacts, while they grow their business by marketing to your contacts too. Be cautious when creating a joint-venture arrangement. Find out about laws in your locality and choose your JV partner wisely.

Finally, your local community will have plenty of people interested in your business who can provide you with support one way or another. Don't close doors behind you and maintain an open mind. Opportunities abound if you are open to considering them.

94. From whom can I drawn inspiration for building my coaching practice?

Coaching, like many professions, offers numerous role models to inspire and motivate you. People who have survived tough economic or other business difficulties can help you face challenges and give you goals to which you can aspire.

Nothing is impossible! Drawing inspiration from others is an excellent tool for building your own coaching practice. These role models generally excel in the coaching world, are brilliant professionals who have overcome adversity or may even be family members and friends.

The important point is to put into practice the survival skills these professionals can share, so as to avoid facing the same pitfalls.

Take a closer look at your circle of influence and your broader circle of contacts. Who do you admire and know? From whom you can learn something relevant to your coaching practice? Now take a look at the broad coaching industry, for example at senior coaches, tutors and peers. Who motivates you with their speeches, seminars, words and actions so you feel ready to take the right steps in your own business? Consider the bigger world. Who lifts your spirit and inspires you?

Once you identify some role models, learn more about them. If a person has written a biography, read it. If possible arrange for a meeting or interview them in person or by phone. Prepare your questions in advance - make sure you benefit from every single minute of that meeting. Once in the meeting, be yourself and let the energy flow between you. It could very well be the beginning of a good friendship!

Drawing inspiration from another is less about their title and position and more about how their attitudes and behaviour influence your own. You can unblock your potential simply by tapping into that source of positive energy. Inspiration and motivation are wonderful and priceless tools that we often neglect to use to the fullest.

One of my sentences I use in my own coaching practice is:

"Let your dreams inspire you!"

Very often we forget these important ingredients for a happier and more balanced life.

95. What are the advantages and disadvantages of a partnership?

Working as a coach can sometimes be a lonely profession. You can easily feel isolated from others. Experienced coaches recommend keeping in touch with the coaching world through coaching support groups, personal development plans, teleclasses, seminars and partnerships.

With regards to partnership, consider these questions:

- What does "partnership" mean to you?
- Why are you considering a partnership as one solution?
- What are the legalities required in your area for establishing a formal partnership?
- How might you choose your partner?
- What might you lose or gain from a partnership?
- How many partners can one have?

Basically, there are two levels for a partnership:

1. The formal and legal partnership;
2. The partnership based on a 'gentlemen's agreement'.

The formal and legal partnership requires following a formal process, similar to setting up a limited company. There are several documents you must become acquainted with, and you will have certain legal and financial responsibilities. I strongly suggest getting legal advice on the subject in order to fully comprehend the formalities and legalities of setting up a formal partnership.

The gentlemen's agreement sounds much simpler but can end up being a headache, especially if your partner doesn't honour the agreement. The gentlemen's agreement partnership is a simple process. Both partners agree on how to split costs and profits or losses, and on how to deal with each individual's networks. Be sure to clarify upfront any issue linked to copyright or intellectual property.

Both partnerships types have a far better chance of surviving and remaining profitable if an accountant and/or lawyer are consulted.

I strongly recommend reflecting upon your reasons for considering a partnership. Whether you need more contacts or seek a stronger resource for professional feedback, these solutions can be achieved by other means. This saves you the hassle of setting up a formal partnership or the trouble that can occur when a partnership is poorly formed.

If after consideration partnership remains the right answer for you, then choosing your partner is the next step. Here both rational and intuitive thinking play important roles. Besides listing all the cons and pros of having X as a partner, such as credibility, communication skills, people skills, coaching skills and competencies, listen to your intuition. It is often dismissed, but it is one of our most important senses.

Before deciding on a partner, coach each other. Be sure your partner is someone from whom you can learn and who will complement your coaching practice. The last thing you want to happen is to be competing with your partner over the ownership of clients.

Depending on the terms of your partnership, you risk sharing all your contacts with your partner, even your current coaching clients. In a partnership where the client can choose the coach you also risk the client deciding to choose your partner over you. For some people this can be devastating to self-esteem and self-confidence.

Some partnerships address this possibility by setting rules about splitting client numbers equally.

In theory you can create many partnerships, especially when they are based on gentlemen's agreements. In practice, more than one partnership can be difficult to manage and increases your risks.

Finally, client and business confidentiality issues must be considered, taking into account the Data Protection Act and other codes of ethics. Also beware of any intellectual property rights that you own.

Below is a list of advantages and disadvantages of partnerships:

Advantages

- You tap into the resources of your partner;
- You tap into your partner's network;
- Clients have the choice to select who they would like as their coach;
- Opportunity to bounce off each other and to discuss ideas;
- Can broaden your horizons;
- You can use the partnership as supervision;
- The partnership can include a co-coaching agreement;
- Costs are split.

Disadvantages

- Profits are split;
- Possibility of conflict or disagreements;
- Clients have the choice to select who they would like as their coach;
- Formalities linked with a legal partnership;
- Can limit your horizons.

96. When should I stop practising pro-bono coaching?

Pro-bono means the services you provide are free. There are a significant number of practitioners outside of coaching who occasionally provide pro-bono services, such as lawyers and therapists. Coaching is no exception.

To offer pro-bono coaching you must be comfortable with the arrangement. If you feel resentment towards the client because you are not being paid, this will damage the coaching relationship and hinder your professionalism, not to mention making it difficult for the client to achieve good results.

Many coaches never provide pro-bono services. Whether you choose to or not is your decision. Some coaches feel uncomfortable with their own level of expertise and therefore find it difficult to ask for certain rates. Fair enough. There is much disparity between coaching rates. Talking with your supervisor, mentor or personal coach may help you understand what is behind your fear and concern.

If you try pro-bono coaching and do not like it, simply stop. You may find you enjoy offering your services pro-bono selectively to truly needy individuals. Again this is a personal decision.

Over time however, as you become more competent and self-confident, you must take a leap of faith. Some coaches take incremental mini-steps. Others take big steps to get closer to their goals. Each coach is different, just as each person is different. What is important is that you are in control and you decide when it is time to make changes.

There are endless stories about coaches all around the world who woke up one day and doubled their rates, just like that, without losing any clients. Whilst this is possible in a non-regulated industry, despite sounding a bit sensational, it may not be ethical or honest. Pay attention to what resonates with you and don't compare yourself to others for competition purposes only: rather seek your own continuous self-development.

97. How can I keep my business costs down?

Coaching does not require a huge investment. In all honesty a pen, a note pad, a telephone line and good skills would set you off as a coach. As with everything, there are different ways of accomplishing the same goals. Therefore, you can plan how to set up your business operations according to your budget and other variables.

The costs of a coaching business are mainly linked to:

- Fixed costs;
- Travelling expenses;
- Marketing;
- Personal development.

Fixed Costs
Fixed costs are always part of setting up and maintaining a business. Fixed costs exist regardless of the number of clients you have. These costs include rent, phone bills, broadband access, electricity bills, stationery, miscellaneous office supplies, etc. To reduce your fixed costs look for better pricing deals. Search online and make comparisons between telephone, broadband and electricity providers, etc. Ask your peers and fellow coaches which contracts they have chosen.

Very seldom do coaches receive clients at their homes, mainly for security and safety reasons. In order to avoid the costs of renting an office, they tend to meet clients at the company's premises, in quiet hotel lobbies or in cafés.

Travelling Expenses
Travelling expenses are most usually reimbursed by the client or his company. However, the odd public transport ticket, a beverage or a meal may be covered by you. Consider all expenses in your hourly rate.

Marketing
The majority of costs associated with operating a coaching business relate to Marketing. In this category there are dozens of free and low cost ideas for reducing costs for both offline and online marketing. Blogs, books and online forums offer endless information on the topic.

- **Free website** – Design your own web pages and receive free hosting in exchange for allowing other businesses to advertise on your web pages. Search online for *free web design sites*;

- **Free business cards** – Design your own business cards with a logo of your choice (or choose from a variety of hundreds of designs.) All of this can be done online in the comfort of your home. Many companies offer free cards up to a specific quantity - you pay for shipping. Search online for *free business cards*;

- **Personalised stationery** – Your business card design vendor will also offer matching stationery. While not a must for your coaching business, you may receive additional discounts because you also ordered business cards. Take advantage of any 'customer specials' you come across;

- **Promote yourself on social media networks** – Create Facebook, Twitter and Linked-in accounts where you can update your status on a regular basis with interesting information that will be seen by your contacts. Participate in online forums with pertinent comments. Include your contact details with a link to your webpage. This will direct traffic to your site;

- **Build your profile** – Speak at events, seminars and workshops organised by your contacts or peers. Typically, coaching support groups look for guest speakers. These are opportunities to build your profile without the usual costs, as well to strengthen your communication skills. Check other events like *Weight Watchers*, which may be looking for inspirational guest speakers;

- **Mailing** - keep in touch with your network at all times. A periodic email will do. However, more and more people despise mass impersonal emailing and prefer personalised direct emails. This is not more than £10 a month and it certainly pays off when one of your contacts decides to purchase your services;

- **Tele-Marketing** – as one of the oldest marketing tools, telephone sales calls can be free if your phone services include unlimited international, national and local calls. Ensure you have a pre-defined script to follow before you embark on tele-marketing, but don't sound stiff. Be in the moment and listen to the person on the other end of the line;

- **Leaflets** – Design and print your own leaflets or flyers and ask to post them in spas and gyms, on notice boards and in places like public libraries where you may find clients;

- **Press releases and ads** – Placing an ad in a newspaper or magazine is very costly. You can always write a short article or include an entry on the 'what's on' section of the newspaper / magazine. Make sure you include your contact details. Don't forget to write to online magazines and e-zines. Posting articles in online directories is one of the top traffic-driving strategies. Search online for *e-zine directories*;

- **Blog** – Creating a blog can be free and provides the opportunity to share your viewpoint and personality with the world. Include links to your homepage if you have a website, and provide contact details at the end of each entry. If your budget allows, semi-custom blog templates are also available for a more distinctive look. Search online for *free Wordpress templates;*

- **Network** – There are free networking events taking place in every town in the world. Obviously, they may not all include your target client group, but you can practise your punch line and elevator speech, as well as making contact with people. Check your local newspaper's events section, or try "Meetups" at www.meetup.com. Consider starting your own group if one is not available;

- **Register with coach directories** – There are coach directories which allow you to register for free, to network with other coaches and to be visible for potential clients seeking a coach. Search online for *coach directory* or *coach finder;*

- **Free phone number** – Set up a free or low-cost 0800 phone number linked to your coaching business telephone number. Search online for *free telephone numbers;*

- **Attend exhibitions** – Exhibitions on wellbeing, health, mind, spirit and body, etc., offer a great opportunity to sell your services and make new contacts. Contact your coaching school or institution where you became accredited to represent them at their exhibition stand.

Personal Development

Personal development costs are probably the highest of all the costs you will incur. However, you can also participate in free seminars and workshops on subjects you want to learn more about. These are normally provided as a teaser with complimentary attendance. After you attend the free event you can decide whether you wish to deepen your subject knowledge.

In addition search online for used books on the subjects of your choice. These are normally one tenth of the cost of a brand new one, and good quality.

98. How far down the line is the best time to increase my coaching rates?

The simplest answer to this question is... *it depends*. It depends on how your coaching has 'matured' and evolved and how you feel about it. In a self-regulated industry there are pricing pressures from everywhere. The strongest of pressures often comes from within your own psyche.

As human beings we tend to compare ourselves with each other constantly. As coaches we often don't escape this behaviour. We compare the rates we charge to peers' rates. More often than not we become frustrated with the realisation that a competitor is charging more and getting it from his clients...particularly frustrating if you feel you are more knowledgeable and/or experienced.

Stop comparing. Your coaching practice is about achieving your personal best, not keeping up with someone else's ideas of how things should be done. Benchmarking is a necessary tool for helping you to get your mind into the proper space. Comparison is merely an evil game that can have drastic consequences for you and the profession. Increasing your rates just because other coaches charge twice as much may damage your reputation and public views about the profession of coaching. Generally, you should be able to charge what the market will bear, as determined by several factors:

- Accreditation;
- Skill;
- Experience;
- Length of practice;
- Type of practice;
- Target audience;
- Coaching quality.

Above all else, value is key. If you turn your practice into a cash machine it will suffer. If you offer each client high quality, value and results, you'll never run out of business.

99. How can I keep my focus when coaching in a recession?

Never is coaching more in demand than during recessionary times. There are two ways to go through a recession: to feel miserable and remain affected by the downturn or to turn the problem into an opportunity and grab it with both hands.

An economic recession is likely to be devastating for a significant proportion of the population. Companies and people focus very hard on reducing costs and expenses and use their time to generate other sources of income. Psychologically speaking, prospects are subdivided into two groups, the ones who believe in coaching and those who are cynical and sceptical about whether coaching can help them with their problems and dilemmas.

For the well-trained coach however, tough times create plenty of opportunities. What is really needed is an ability to adapt to the economy and to modify one's sales strategies in order to continue to create a good source of revenue. This adaptability means you will never be out of work, no matter what the economic climate. All you must do is change what you sell, change to whom you sell it and change how you sell it.

It is simple, but not necessarily easy. You must be resilient and persistent.

Changing What You Sell

Here we define these changes as diversification. If you've been strictly offering in-person, phone or Skype coaching sessions, these and other options should be explored:

- Audio products;
- Videos;
- Workshops;
- Books;
- Booklets;
- Teleclasses;
- Webinars;
- Weekend retreats.

Changing to Whom You Sell

Broaden your client portfolio by thinking 'outside the box'. Even if you are a specialist coach you can always turn to more general subjects. You might rebrand yourself and your practice to suit topics currently on the mind of the public, such as career coaching or transition coaching.

If your clients are generally corporations, consider branching out to SMEs (small to medium enterprises) or even to sole proprietorships, or vice-versa. There are coaches who approach the public sector and governmental institutions as a way to broaden their client portfolio. Get in touch with previous clients, as well as your networking contacts and other members of your circle of influence. Get involved in social media to expand your online visibility.

Changing how you sell

How you sell your services and products can also be modified. Consider:

- Up-selling;
- Economies of scale (pay one-get-two type of campaigns);
- Monthly rates instead of hourly rates;
- Packages instead of paying per session;
- Themed packages, such as transition management, stress management or time management, instead of loose sessions;
- Referral programmes.

In a recession, the important thing is to remain loyal to your own core values and to be as imaginative as possible. During a recession people are desperate to be rescued and to ease their situations. If you can provide this ethically, you have found your way through tough times.

100. When does 'going international' become appropriate?

The beauty of the coaching profession is that you choose to do business whenever, wherever and with whoever you wish. Coaching isn't restricted to a time zone or a geographical area, which makes the expression 'going international' obsolete. With the latest technology you can work from the comfort of your home while coaching someone who lives in a different continent.

Some coaches with advanced linguistic skills coach over the telephone or Internet (e.g., using Skype) in different languages with clients in different countries. However, nothing prevents you from taking a flight and visiting your client for face-to-face coaching. The expenses incurred are normally paid by the client.

The coach must have good mastery of his coaching skills in order to provide an excellent service via the telephone or Skype. Your coaching skills, competence, rapport and trustworthiness are reasons why a client would choose you, on the other side of the planet, over another coach down their own street.

For some aspiring coaches, leaving their local coaching 'nest' may be a major step. A new coach should expand his comfort zone slowly. No one will force you to take on more clients. To be frank, you are likely to be the one who will want to enlarge your client portfolio and telephone coaching will open the door to many new opportunities.

Tapping into this world of opportunities could also mean a better quality of life for you. Your income will continue to increase as you take on clients across the planet. You can live anywhere you choose as long as you have telephone and broadband connections. Nowadays for a small monthly fee you can get VoIP (Voice over Internet) services and add a local phone number to your technical hardware. Your clients pay the cost of a local call and you answer from wherever you are in the world without disclosing your location. The world becomes your oyster!

In summary, going international can begin on day one of your business life, as it can on any other day. It's your choice.

101. What is the best approach to building my coaching business?

This may sound like a strange question, but many aspiring coaches don't know how to start building a coaching business. They often become overwhelmed and feel pulled in many different directions.

Two of the most important entrepreneurial traits are patience and persistence. Building a coaching business, or any business, requires much patience at every single step, from dealing with governmental agencies to managing suppliers. Persistence is important for holding you up through tough times when there are not yet enough clients. This will place you in a good position to think creatively about other ways to boost your business and to make adjustments quickly as needed.

I believe the best coaching businesses spring from heartfelt passion. It certainly sounds strange to bring matters of the heart into a rational topic, but once you come across the feeling that you have "come home", your dreams and desires are more easily attainable.

When you set up your business there will be plenty of people ready to tell you what to do, who to follow and when to do what. You will hear plenty of *shoulds, have tos and musts.* Expert advice has its place, but in the end you must follow your own instincts. Ponder the advice, think about the consequences of doing things your way, and listen to the option that most resonates with you. It's your business - the one which you will wake up to every day - so make it one that will inspire you and give you positive energy. If you don't think a certain piece of advice or tip makes sense for your journey, don't take it.

Often beginners get so excited with setting up their own business that they forget to think. Or they may think too much, out of fear. This is simply 'planning the plan' and can create missed opportunities. As with everything, the answer lies with balance. Deep inside you have the answers. Be honest with yourself in every step of the way.

I strongly recommend that you apply the principles of self-coaching in developing your coaching practice. Make use of coaching sessions with peers, co-coaching and maybe even a mentor if necessary. Learning from others' experiences is very good, even though sometimes you need to experiment for yourself in order to evolve and to move on.

I guarantee that following your heart is a worthwhile approach. When you feel right, you do right!

Appendix

International Professional Coaching Bodies Contact Details

Association for Coaching – AC

Email: enquiries@associationforcoaching.com

Website: www.associationforcoaching.com

European Mentoring & Coaching Council

Email: EMCC.Administrator@emccouncil.org

Website: www.emccouncil.org

International Coaching Federation – ICF

Email: icfheadquarters@coachfederation.org

Website: www.coachfederation.org

International Institute of Coaching – IIC

Email: accreditation@the-iic.org

Website: www.internationalinstituteofcoaching.org

Bibliography

Academy of Executive Coaching, Notebooks,www.aoec.com, London, 2009.

Barber, J., *Good Question*. Great Britain: Bookshaker, 2005.

Barosa-Pereira, A. *Coaching em Portugal - Teoria e Prática*. Lisbon: Edições Sílabo, 2008.

Catalão, J. A. e Penim, A.T., *Ferramentas de Coaching*. Lisbon: Lidel Edições Técnicas Ltd, 2010.

Chapman, P., *The Pocket Life Coach*, Crown House Publishing Limited, 2008.

Covey, S., *7 Habits of Highly Effective People*. London: Simon & Schuster UK Ltd, 2004.

Covey, S., *The 8th Habit*. London: Simon & Schuster UK Ltd, 2004.

Dalai Lama, Cutler, H., *The Art of Happiness*. London: Hodder & Soughton, 1998.

Dodd, P. and Sundheim, D., *The 25 best time management tools and techniques*. USA: Capstone, 2008

Downey, M., *Effective Coaching - Lessons from the coach's coach*. (2nd Edition) USA: Cengage Learning, 2003.

Landsberg, M., *The Tao of Coaching – Boost your effectiveness at work by inspiring and developing those around you*. London: Profile Books, 2003.

Leary-Joyce J., *Gestalt Coaching Handbook, e-book from* www.aoec.com 2010

Martin, C., *The Life Coaching Handbook*. Gales: Crown House Publishing Ltd, 2001.

Metcalf, L., *The Miracle question – answer it and change your life*. Gales: Crown House Publishing Ltd, 2009

Miles, A., *Coaching Practice*. Leeds: Coachwise Business Solutions, 2004.

Noble Manhattan Coaching, *Practitioner Coaching Modules*. Weymouth, 2007.

O'Neil, M., *Executive Coaching with Backbone and Heart – A systems approach to engaging leaders with their challenges*. (2nd Edition) San Francisco: Jossey-Bass, 2007.

Pemberton, C., *Coaching to Solutions – A Manager's Toolkit for Performance Delivery*. Oxford: Butterworth-Heinemann, 2006.

Simmons, A., *Mindfulness and Meditation – Coaching readiness... for the coach*. choice – the magazine of professional Coaching, Volume 5, Number 4. USA, 2007.

Sullivan, W. e Rees, J., *Clean Language - Revealing Metaphors and Opening Minds*. Gales: Crown House Publishing Limited, 2008.

Whitmore, J., *Coaching for Performance, GROWing human potential and purpose. The principles and practice of Coaching and leadership*. (4th Edition) London: Nicholas Brealey Publishing, 2009.

Whitworth, L., Kimsey-House, K., Kimsey-House, H., e Sandahl, P., *Co-active Coaching: News skills for Coaching people toward success in work and life*. (2nd Edition) USA: Davies-Black Publishing, 2007.

Index

A

Accreditation xi, xvi, xvii, 15, 17, 19, 37, 38, 39, 45, 47, 49, 50, 57, 112, 199, 219
Affirmations 145

B

Benefits xi, 3, 6, 7, 8, 23, 32, 37, 48, 51, 80, 122, 125, 186, 193, 196
Body language 22, 23, 25, 71, 85, 89, 91, 103, 118, 120, 135, 137, 152
Business coaching 5, 45, 181

C

Cancellations xi, 43
Categories xi, 5, 117
Clean Language 25, 57, 101, 136, 153, 222
Coaching career ix, xii, 57, 72
Coaching model xii, 41, 73, 74, 75, 82, 123, 129, 131, 171, 185
Confidentiality xi, xiii, 31, 32, 35, 50, 51, 93, 111, 112, 113, 143, 171, 204
Contract xi, 35, 41, 42, 43, 187
Costs xiv, 5, 9, 32, 146, 155, 177, 189, 203, 207, 208, 209, 213

D

Dream list xii, 81, 82

E

Emotions 9, 11, 23, 25, 72, 85, 127, 147
Engagement xi, xii, 29, 41, 42, 51, 63, 65, 66, 93, 112, 139, 170, 171, 172
Ethics xi, xv, xvii, 1, 31, 33, 37, 39, 41, 43, 51, 111, 112, 131, 139, 143, 204
Executive coaching xii, 5, 9, 19, 45, 46, 61, 93, 113, 171, 179

F

Face-to-face coaching xii, 103, 215
Facial expressions 103, 165
Focus xiv, 3, 22, 23, 25, 71, 72, 75, 77, 79, 87, 99, 133, 146, 165, 170, 171, 172, 179, 183, 213
Forbidden territories xii, 31, 42, 47, 107, 131

G

Goals 3, 7, 8, 29, 32, 51, 61, 66, 74, 75, 79, 81, 82, 93, 106, 109, 123, 125, 140, 145, 161, 170, 201, 205, 207
Goal setting xii, 5, 75, 77, 81, 82
Grow xiv, xvi, 74, 177, 191, 199

H

Hesitation 22, 85, 165
Homework xiii, 113, 119, 123, 124, 181

I

Improvement 13, 19, 47, 48, 49, 63, 159, 172
Inspiration xiv, 9, 19, 122, 169, 170, 179, 201
internal dialogue xiii, xvi, 12, 24, 25, 133, 134, 167
Intuition xiii, 6, 19, 22, 25, 58, 60, 63, 71, 74, 75, 83, 85, 103, 125, 136, 141, 161, 162, 163, 165, 166, 167, 169, 170, 199, 204

L

Learning xii, xvi, 15, 17, 57, 74, 95, 96, 97, 99, 102, 159, 165, 173
Life coaching 5, 6, 27, 45, 103, 193
Listening xvi, 6, 11, 19, 22, 25, 65, 72, 83, 87, 96, 103, 114, 118, 127, 133, 141, 161, 169

M

Marketing 13, 67, 180, 191, 195, 199, 207, 208
Mentoring xvii, 9, 13, 37, 219
Metaphors 135, 153, 222
Mistakes xii, 71, 72, 77, 196

N

Niche xiv, 17, 177, 179, 180, 181, 193
NLP xii, 57, 82, 97, 99, 100, 145, 146, 147

P

Partnership xiv, 177, 199, 203, 204
Preparation xi, 21, 22, 23, 87, 103, 111, 131, 162
Pro-bono xiv, 29, 49, 109, 159, 187, 205
Professional Coaching Bodies 219
Psychotherapy xi, 11, 12

Q

Qualification 15, 19, 50, 112
Questioning 19, 25, 65, 102, 105, 118, 119, 121, 133, 146, 161, 162, 165, 167, 169

R

Rapport xiii, 11, 19, 53, 65, 99, 101, 103, 122, 137, 138, 141, 154, 161, 215

Rates xiv, 45, 46, 49, 177, 190, 193, 205, 211, 214
Recession xiv, 213, 214
Referrals xii, 53, 54, 66, 181, 191
Reframing 82, 145
Report 93, 143, 163, 190
ROI 41, 61, 62

S

Saboteur 175
Scaling xiii, 157, 172
Self-coaching xiii, 167, 179, 217
Self-esteem xiii, 5, 7, 123, 149, 151, 152, 167, 175, 204
Self-management 25, 47, 71, 72, 103, 107, 111, 131
Services vii, xiv, 6, 15, 27, 29, 31, 33, 45, 46, 51, 54, 61, 67, 113,
         127, 139, 149, 170, 177, 181, 185, 187, 188, 189, 190,
         191, 193, 195, 196, 197, 205, 208, 209, 214, 215
Session xi, xii, xiii, xvi, 3, 5, 7, 11, 21, 22, 23, 25, 27, 43, 45, 46,
         47, 48, 51, 53, 54, 69, 71, 72, 73, 74, 75, 79, 81, 83, 87,
         91, 100, 102, 103, 111, 112, 113, 114, 115, 119, 121, 122,
         123, 125, 126, 127, 129, 130, 131, 133, 134, 135, 139,
         141, 153, 154, 157, 161, 163, 165, 170, 171, 172, 173,
         185, 188, 193, 196, 214
Silence 23, 71, 83, 85, 103, 127, 136, 151, 169, 172
Skills xiii, xix, 3, 4, 11, 14, 15, 17, 19, 25, 33, 45, 47, 51, 55, 57,
         63, 65, 66, 72, 73, 74, 82, 83, 96, 103, 105, 109, 115, 125,
         133, 140, 141, 159, 161, 165, 167, 169, 173, 174, 175,
         179, 184, 185, 186, 187, 188, 189, 201, 204, 207, 208,
         215, 222
Sponsor xii, 9, 29, 41, 63, 93
Standards xi, xvii, xix, 17, 31, 33, 35, 37, 39, 54, 151
Supervision xi, xvi, 1, 4, 17, 35, 37, 38, 47, 48, 49, 50, 91, 97, 111,
         112, 170, 184, 204

T

Taking notes xiii, 113
Telephone coaching xii, 85, 103, 112, 113, 114, 159, 173, 193,
         215
Testimonial xii, 55, 185
Tonality 118, 137, 167

U

Up-selling 190, 214

V

Values xii, xvi, 5, 14, 19, 31, 32, 46, 67, 72, 80, 81, 105, 106, 129,
         169, 214